I SEE BY MY GET-UP

DATE DUE

~~MY 27 '99~~			
~~JE 10 09~~			

DEMCO 38-296

Ron Querry, 1948

R

I See by
My Get-Up

Ron Querry

WITH PHOTOGRAPHS BY ELAINE QUERRY
FOREWORD BY LARRY L. KING

UNIVERSITY OF OKLAHOMA PRESS

Norman and London

...eir good working cow dogs
...appreciation and affection

Portions of this book were previously published, in slightly different form, as follows:

Chapters 4, 6, 7, 9, 14, 15 and 16 in the *Dallas Times Herald* as "Southwest Letters" (revised versions of Chapter 7 later appeared in *Speedhorse* and *The Sentinel*); Chapter 5 in the *Albuquerque Journal*'s "Impact Magazine" as "The Way to a Lady's Heart," and Chapter 10 in "Impact Magazine" as "I See by My Get-Up That I Am a Cowboy"; and Chapters 6, 12 and 16 in *Livestock Market Digest* as "Home on the Range."

Library of Congress Cataloging-in-Publication Data

Querry, Ronald B. (Ronald Burns), 1943–
    I see by my get-up / Ron Querry ; with photographs by Elaine Querry ; foreword by Larry L. King.
        p.   cm.
    Originally published: Albuquerque : University of New Mexico Press, c1987. With new afterword.
    ISBN 0–8061–2638–8
    1. Querry, Ronald B. (Ronald Burns), 1943–
2. Ranch life—New Mexico.   3. Ranchers—New Mexico—Biography.   I. Title.
    [SF194.2.Q47A3   1994]
    978.9'25053'092—dc20
    [B]   93-38190
                                                                  CIP

Published by the University of Oklahoma Press, Norman, Publishing Division of the University. Copyright ©1987 by Ron Querry. New Afterword copyright ©1994 by Ron Querry. All rights reserved. Manufactured in the U.S.A. First printing of the University of Oklahoma Press edition, 1994.

1 2 3 4 5 6 7 8 9 10

Contents

"I see by your get-up that you are a cowboy"—
These words he did say as I boldly walked by;
Come sit down beside me and hear my sad story;
I'm shot in the breast and I know I must die.

The Streets of Laredo
Traditional

I SEE BY MY GET-UP

Foreword

RIGHT AWAY, I INSIST ON CLAIMING credit for this book.

No, I didn't write it: Ron Querry did. No, I didn't take the photographs gracing it: Miss Elaine did. Neither did I sell, buy, edit or publish the manuscript: folks at the University of New Mexico had the good taste and foresight to accomplish those things. And now the University of Oklahoma has taken up the cause with this fine new edition.

But I am as proud as the proverbial peacock to have been the fellow who *suggested* this book about a decade ago, based on a few personal letters from Dr. Querry and a couple of articles he had published in Dallas and Albuquerque newspapers chronicling the uncertainties of making an abrupt transition from college professor to would-be rancher despite his owning feet of the tenderest sort. As one who had knocked about the literary world for a quarter-century, I fancied I knew a story when I saw one—especially as Dr. Querry's had the potential to offer much laughter and a few tears, courtship and marriage, struggles against the elements promising here a victory and there a defeat, to say nothing of critters (both four-legged and two-legged) equipped to be sometimes lovable, sometimes irascible and sometimes downright mean. I am delighted with the results. Hereafter all cheers should be reserved for Dr. Querry; but first, let's hear it for my perspicacity without which you would not be holding his book in your hand while poised on the brink of a good reading adventure.

Ron Querry was not yet "Dr. Querry" when I first met him at the Oklahoma City airport about twelve years ago; nor was he the personal friend, semi-cowboy or author he has become. He was, instead, an English teacher who had lured me to speak at the University of Oklahoma through a combination of shameless flattery about my own writing and the offer of a thousand dollar fee plus expenses. Not that I then needed the money: I had lucked into co-authoring the hit musical comedy, *The Best Little Whorehouse in Texas,* which then was playing all over America and much of the world. With the scurvy financial monkey of the free-lance writer off my back at long last, I was lying fallow professionally and lying to my new wife about how much I drank. In short, when Ron Querry's letter arrived I was looking to leap the fence and enthusiastically relax myself in a distant meadow unobserved. Some undefinable, unspoken something in Ron Querry's letter seemed to indicate that neither he nor his friends would attempt to hobble my social instincts. Again—as with the notion for this book—my perspicacity proved near-perfect. Within two hours Querry, King and assorted academic and newspaper consorts had joined the Oklahoma Feed and Grain Association (which had the bad luck to be in convention just off the hotel-lobby bar where we had paused for lengthy refreshments) and I had puzzled the assembled feed-growers and feed-sellers by delivering to them—unbidden—much of the speech that had been slated for the ears of OU intellectuals. Ron Querry was such a good sport about this unexpected turn of events that I immediately claimed him as a fast friend. Later that night, in a Norman beer joint, I bestowed upon him his Doctorate with all the appreciation for higher education that a dazed high-school dropout could muster.

Dr. Querry soon quit teaching, and I soon quit drinking. (Though, to be honest, neither was offered options.) He began writing letters of slow days spent reading and dreaming in a primitive New Mexico ranch house fallen into disrepair, days marred only by the occasional need to kill rattlesnakes or tote drinking water from distant reaches. But beneath those idyllic reports of the rustic life there ran an undercurrent of loneliness, of worries about money and of the professional future. Soon there came an upbeat lilt in Dr. Querry's dispatches: he had met a lovely, lovely rancher lady who had threatened his heart on sight; before a decent interval elapsed, there arrived a wedding picture of Dr. Querry and his bride—Miss Elaine—who was, indeed, as double lovely as advertised. Appended was a euphoric note bearing the stunning news that the former college professor had become an instant big-time rancher. As Mark Twain said of a premature report of his own death, that bit of news would soon prove to be "greatly exaggerated."

Subsequent letters revealed—as does *I See by My Get-Up*—that Dr. Querry was, in truth, an apprentice hand on a hardscrabble ranch and that he approached his new role harboring a Walter Mittyish view of himself as the old bedroll cowpoke incarnate: part John Wayne, part Larry Mahan, perhaps part Zane Grey. His scholar's sensibilities, however, soon permitted the neophyte "big time rancher" to realize that more experienced cattlemen perhaps viewed him as more nearly a cross between Dale Evans and Mister Peepers. Word was being muttered among true cowpokes, you see, that the fledgling rancher amounted to no more than an ex-school teacher who aspired to be a doggone *writer*: occupations, I know from my background as a child of West Texas, that in the more sparsely settled precincts of the American Southwest are somehow automatically bracketed with hairdressers and pie-makers. To clear his name of the charge that he was fit for little but "woman's work" my friend had to learn cowboy techniques well enough to survive or, forevermore, reap the community's scorn.

Dr. Querry's private letters first introduced me to many of the characters and critters now populating this book: Lefty, the cow dog who often wasn't; a calf named Trouble because he was nothing but; Moonshine and Rumshop and Comet, horses all, who acted insulted when ridden or worked; Gypsy, the reluctant mama cow who abandoned her offspring at birth; other cows who kicked when milked, horses who kicked when shod, dogs who killed chickens and bravely barked at horned toads but who kept a respectful distance and a discreet silence when in the presence of dangerous rattlesnakes. I laughed, as you shall, when Dr. Querry's first attempt to operate a "squeeze chute" during branding led to his inadvertently choking a breeder bull so that, forever after, the bull—while not at all disadvantaged in the art of putting cows in a family way—otherwise acted so stupid he was christened "Retardo Montalbull." And I laughed, if sympathetically, at other mishaps as my friend adapted to range life by trial and error. I met, too, in these letters, an enterprising good-old-boy and son of the soil, A. T., who gamely assisted Dr. Querry through his cowboy apprenticeship with many sighs and hopeless head shakes; a hard-eyed banker who practiced usury without blushing; the ghost of a noble old rancher, George Bibb, who had been Miss Elaine's grandfather and whose traditions she stubbornly carried on; tourists who invaded a cattle roundup to spook and booger four-legged critters unaccustomed to clicking Nikon cameras and clouds of French perfume.

I don't recall at what exact point the little light went off in my head and I thought, *Ol' Doc Querry's got hisself the makings of a damn good book here!* I fired off a letter demanding that my friend begin said book upon receipt. He did not resist, but immediately called to describe me as a genius and then quickly commenced humming, whistling and typing. I am sure that like all writers going hammer-and-tongs at a first book, Dr. Querry had private visions of riches, Pulitzer or Nobel Prizes and partying in Hollywood with Johnny Carson after making his debut on the *Tonight Show.* Writers somehow live in fantasylands even when they are writing true slices of life. Sometimes I think, indeed, that fantasies are the most important fuel available to keep writers going.

From my own experiences and the tales of other writers who˙ had survived their first big literary wars, I knew there would come a time when Dr. Querry's initial soaring enthusiasm would drop like a concrete airplane from his euphoric sky. There would be days when the words wouldn't come, when no amount of ordering them could make them parade across the page in satisfactory formation. Days when Dr. Querry would sulk and maybe even unfairly snap at the innocent Miss Elaine, nights when he would cry out in the dark for his mother, times when he would write me or call me to snivel and whine and protest that he couldn't finish the goddamned book and perhaps berate me for having put him in such a hopeless fix. All of that more or less happened.

Sometimes I secretly wanted to hug the struggling, tormented budding author—because I, too, had mired in those uncertain airless bogs he felt trapped in. But knowing that no writer is truly ever short of sympathy for himself, I hardened my heart and threatened and goaded Dr. Querry as editors and more experienced writers had treated my own early panic attacks. "Hush up all that sniveling and whining, Doctor," I ordered. "Nobody promised you a goddurned rose garden. You've just got to keep typing through your troubles until you come out on the other side. *Go write your damned book!*" Then I would threaten to strangle my friend should I hear another peep from him before he had accomplished at least one more chapter, and quickly hung up before he could return my abuse. Friends sure do come in handy sometimes.

Midway in writing, the ranch life Miss Elaine had long lived and loved (and that Dr. Querry obviously was learning to love) suddenly became threatened. For a time this book also appeared threatened. Would it even be completed in the face of the new adversity? Would the book, originally conceived as a comic adventure, be the same should Ron and Elaine lose their ranch? *Would* they lose the ranch? In the interest of drama and Dr. Querry's tale, I will say only that the first question obviously should be answered in the affirmative because the book is now in your hands.

While I know that subsequent developments caused much pain to the author, and to the help-mate who took the photographs, I believe that events as ultimately played out actually helped *I See By My Get-Up* become a better book. It would have been a good tale in any case; but the unexpected has made it a book of more depth, more of real life. Anger came into it, and sadness, and resentment, and uncertainty—and, yes, after all the noise and trouble came a quiet new strength.

That Ron Querry could adapt his work to the unexpected and unwelcome developments, instinctively exploiting them for purposes of his art, gives me a great deal of assurance that we haven't heard the last of him as a writer. He has the instincts, and the strength, to persevere. Next time, by golly, I bet *nobody* has to suggest he write a book.

Larry L. King
Washington, D.C.
September 1993

(Larry L. King is the author to date of eleven books, six stage plays, two filmscripts, several television documentaries and numerous magazine articles. He has won the Helen Hayes Award and the Theater Lobby Award for his stage plays, the Stanley Walker Journalism Award for general excellence in reporting, and a television Emmy for documentary writing. In addition, Mr. King has been nominated for a National Book Award and a Broadway Tony.)

Introduction

WHEN I BEGAN WRITING WHAT WAS
eventually to become this book, my intention was that the
work should be a kind of *exercise* for me—not unlike jogging or
Jazzercise. (I don't want to give you the impression right here at
the outset that I'm some kind of health freak who eats twigs
and seaweed and jogs every morning—truth is, I'm allergic to
natural foods and have always made it a point to break into a
run only on those infrequent occasions when I perceive something big and hairy chasing me.) You see, I imagined that the
mere act of writing would help keep the left side of my brain
firm and fit. (Or is it the right side? I never can remember
which one is supposed to be in charge of the cognitive skills
like reading and writing.)

It seems I've always faced this dilemma: Whenever I find myself doing the kind of thing for which my formal schooling has
prepared me—namely teaching college English—I worry over
the fact that I'm not engaging in the kind of "manly" endeavor
that I imagine a person must perform in order legally to be paid
the minimum wage. I get to figuring that maybe all those
"good ol' boys" I've come across around feedlots and cow out-
fits who've dealt me no small amount of what I mostly took to
be good-natured ribbing over the years for being an egghead

professor—or, as they like to say, "a school marm"—might just be right. At least I'll confess that they struck a nerve.

Of course, the opposite is true, as well. On those other occasions, when I've found myself happily sweating over, say, the shoeing or the training and breeding of horses, I've suffered genuine feelings of guilt associated with the notion that I'm wasting a fine and expensive college education by performing "common labor." It's as though I can hear my mother's voice telling me: "Use your mind, son, or you're gonna lose it."

Anyway, I began work on this book as a form of mental aerobics a couple of years back because it had become clear to me that I'd sure enough settled on the work that was to engage me for the rest of my life, or at least until my heart attacked me or I got shipped off to the Home.

I had a vision that fate intended me to be a big-time cattle rancher. And as such, I was destined to spend the rest of my days riding the range—both in the saddle and in the pickup. I reckoned I'd forevermore be doing *cowboy* things: Things like listening to cattle low softly, chasing ornery little dogies ("Get Along!"), wrestling steers (good-naturedly of course), riding fence (in pleasantly warm and dry weather, I imagined), strumming guitars, and kissing horses . . . that sort of thing.

Still, those old feelings of guilt kept creeping around my head. I mean, I couldn't just *forget* that I'd spent half my life in college classrooms—as a student and as a teacher. Besides, I figured I owed it to literate America (not to mention my mother) to reveal the story of how it was I went—practically overnight—from effete college professor to apprentice cow puncher and finally on to rich cattle baron.

Here was a story with all the sure-fire ingredients of a classic Grade B Western Movie:

The Handsome Cowboy rides alone across the high prairie. He calls no single place home. His yellow Toyota pickup and his faithful little blue cow dog are his only companions.

Unknown to the Handsome Cowboy, on this same high prairie lives the Beautiful Young Rancher Lady, struggling alone and against all odds to hold onto her beloved and recently departed grandfather's cattle ranch in spite of evil, underhanded attempts to evict her from her rightful home.

[*Black Clouds Gather Overhead.*] Then, just when things appear hopeless, the Handsome Cowboy rides up [*Cut to Blinding Snowstorm*] to the delapidated barn where the Beautiful Young Rancher Lady is weeping softly over the still-warm carcass of her favorite little calf.

Time passes. [*Pages of Calendar Are Seen Turning.*]

The Beautiful Young Rancher Lady and The Handsome Cowboy fall in love. [*Cut to BYRL and HC Bashfully Holding Hands.*]

Together they repair the falling-down fences and the rusted old windmill. The terrible drouth finally breaks and lush green grass grows belly-high in the pastures. [*Cut to Playful Calves and Frisky Colts Gamboling Through Meadow.*]

The ranch becomes, once more, the joyous and prosperous place that it had once been [*Flowers Blooming and Birds Singing*]. The cattle are tame and gentle, contentedly chewing their cuds—they no longer get sick or die.

The Handsome Couple lives happily ever after. [*Melodious Violin and Cello Music Plays. Fade to Beautiful Sunset.*]

Anyhow, that's the way it was *supposed* to happen. But listen. . . .

ONE

My Heroes Ain't Always Been Cowboys

SOME OF MY MOST POWERFUL MEMORIES have to do with that period in my life when I was an honest-to-god cowboy.

Mind you, I'm not talking here about your Plastic or Cosmic Cowboy. And I'm sure as heck not talking about your Urban Cowboy who just kind of fell in with the rest of America behind New Jersey's own John Travolta when he two-stepped his way across the silver screen. No indeed, I really *did* used to ride mean broncs and rope sorry steers. And yes, I used to brand and castrate the little he-calves and dribble chewing tobacco down my chin and walk all bent over 'cause I was so stove-up. *Damn,* it was just a wonderful time!

Of course it wasn't always like that . . . I wasn't *always* a cowboy. I can remember back when I used to be a regular person, and my life was just like everybody else's. Like the time when I was a freshman in college and one of my professors gave the whole class the finger.

It was 1964, and I had successfully petitioned the Commandant of the United States Marine Corps to discharge me a few weeks prior to my scheduled release date so that I might prepare for some yet to be determined—but clearly *un*military— career by enrolling as a full-time student at what was then called San Francisco State College.

5

It was an English class, and what the professor was doing, he said, was teaching us about the different forms of communication. Giving us the finger was his example of nonverbal communication. The man's name was T. Mike Walker, and I can clearly recall that he was dressed in a white shirt and maroon tie, a gray herringbone jacket with leather elbow patches, and a pair of faded Levis. (The faded Levis was the remarkable thing about his outfit. I had been raised in Oklahoma, the state where Oral Roberts would later build his City of Faith and namesake university with $48-a-square-foot love offerings; it had never occurred to me that a college professor might actually show up for work wearing a shirt and tie with bluejeans.) Walker told us he had worked as a police officer for the city of San Francisco, but had undergone either a schizophrenic episode or a divine revelation when called upon to spend an afternoon arresting demonstrators on the steps of the federal building wherein the House Un-American Activities Committee was meeting, when all *morning* he'd carried a sign and yelled ugly remarks at duly elected officials in front of that same building. (I don't figure I need to point out that an English teacher at San Francisco State College in 1964 who wore bluejeans to class and made obscene gestures at his freshmen students was not exactly one of your right-wing ultra-conservative individuals. As to the reason why the man worked part-time as a police officer, subsequent experience has taught me that as a college English teacher he needed the extra money.)

Anyway, when T. Mike Walker gave me the finger that day more than twenty years ago, I knew right away that what I wanted to be in my life was a professional college person . . . a professor of English.

In those days, if you had a Ph.D.—even in English—from any halfway respectable university (as opposed to the ones that come highly recommended in ads on matchbook covers) you simply applied to a few colleges for teaching positions and then accepted the best offer as to money or the most attractive place to live—depending on your priorities. But by the time I finally finished my Ph.D.—twelve years later—teaching jobs were scarce.

I bounced around for a few years. I taught literature to kidnappers and murderers inside the walls of the New Mexico State Penitentiary—I got to go home at night. I taught wealthy young preppies at a fancy private women's college up in Ohio. I directed a USAID program for oily-skinned Arab students who, only later did I discover, went on to use their good American college educations *not* to fight Communism and practice free enterprise in their native lands like the U.S. government intended, but rather to become terrorist hijackers and embassy bomb chunkers. And I worked for a while as an editor for a slick trade magazine devoted to Quarter Horse racing run by a couple of obnoxious women who seemed untroubled by the fact that they didn't know the front end of a horse from the back. In between these jobs, I worked as a horseshoer, a trainer, a riding instructor, a breeding farm manager, and a stall mucker.

In fact, I was working on a Thoroughbred breeding farm in New Mexico when my brother broke a long-standing tradition and got in touch with me. Chris, having apparently learned nothing from seeing the total lack of lucrative teaching opportunities available to his highly educated senior sibling, was working on a liberal arts doctorate while slaving as a graduate assistant at the University of Oklahoma. He told me that the big-shot administrators at OU had mysteriously and suddenly gotten rich and were fixing to hire about a dozen new English teachers—something about wanting to have an academic program the football team could be proud of. Chris said he figured I might just be tired enough of real horse shit to go back for another helping of the kind produced in the halls of academe.

I wrote up a fairly accurate curriculum vitae; by that I mean I did not award myself any high honors or degrees from Harvard, nor claim to be a co-recipient of the Nobel Peace Prize . . . although I'll admit to having substituted a collection of fictitious grants and obscure fellowships for several of my hand-to-mouth stall-mucker periods. Then I wrote up a letter of application with fairly good spelling and decent enough punctuation and mailed them off to OU.

I never heard back from anyone in authority personally. About two weeks before the semester was to start, however, Chris called—collect—to say that as far as he could tell, I'd been hired. Some secretary in the English Department office had alertly noticed that I had written my Master's thesis on the radical Black poet and playwright LeRoi Jones, and had even published a couple of articles in respectable Afro-American Studies journals. By coincidence, the department's token Black person had decided at the last minute not to return to teaching, thus leaving the obligatory Afro-American Literature course without an instructor. The entire English Department faculty had been canvased but no one would volunteer to take over the class; all *I* had to do to become a card-carrying member of the OU faculty was show up and sign a solemn oath that I would never attempt to overthrow the government of the United States of America or the state of Oklahoma.

When I walked into my assigned classroom on that warm September morning in 1979, I was dressed—as I have always dressed for the first day of class—in a white shirt and tie, a gray herringbone jacket, and faded Levis. Assuming a studied pro-fessorial demeanor, I looked out into the faces of my class to observe thirty-six very large American Negro men and one di-minutive Choctaw Indian girl. The males, mostly fullbacks and strong-side tackles imported to campus from truck farms and bayous in Texas and Louisiana by the head football coach to help protect his job and his Heisman Trophy candidate's knees, regarded their honkey professor with sullen silence. (The Indian girl later confided that she had ended up in the wrong room, understandably—if mistakenly—assuming mine to be the meet-ing place of the Sports in Literature class she had fancied.) Ob-viously, the large gentlemen in the room that morning had been expecting someone other than a nattily attired white boy to provide their academic leadership. Reading their amazed, amused, and angry faces, I knew I had to seize the moment or lose the day.

"What it *is*," I said, in my best jive patois. "This morning we're going to study some of the various forms of communication."

And then I gave them the finger.

I made it through that first year as the University's Black Literature specialist without traumatic incidents. Then the following year the department scored a minor coup and marginally satisfied the administration's affirmative action officer by recruiting an actual person of color to take over my role. He was a native of some emerging African country, a graduate of a fancy Ivy League school, and had a slight speech impediment. Although I hadn't seen a powder blue leisure suit with contrasting white stitching in years, he was a pretty snappy dresser. He had a biblical name and a tendency to faint during his lectures. (Although it was rumored that these fainting spells were the result of chronic low blood sugar coupled with the lack of a nutritious breakfast, further complicated by a voodoo curse that had been laid on him back home, I never did learn the official diagnosis of his condition.)

While still a candidate for his position, Professor Noah LummBooley was brought to campus for the traditional wining and dining, interviewing and showing off. As I was considered *the* person in the Department most in touch with the "Negro Community," I was called upon for advice in matters of style and social behavior attendant to Dr. LummBooley's visit.

The chairman, planning an intimate formal dinner for the candidate and a couple of college deans, asked me—in all seriousness—if it wouldn't be proper for his wife to serve fried chicken and collard greens, or should they play it safe and order up some barbecued ribs? I was relieved that it was winter and watermelon was not yet in season.

After one year at OU, LummBooley was hired away by some effete Eastern college—a move which caused considerable uproar seeing as how Noah had failed to mention he was look-

9

ing to better himself so quickly. Such was his haste that he moved out of his apartment in Norman and reported to his new workplace without thinking to notify OU administrators.

For the first two weeks of the fall semester, our harried department chairman dispatched his secretary each morning to post a series of notices in Noah's classroom:

> Due to an unexpected death in his family,
> Professor LummBooley will not be here *today only.*

or:

> Dr. LummBooley is well on the road to recovery—
> He'll be here tomorrow, *for sure!*

In truth, no one had any idea where the man was.

When it finally became clear that LummBooley had, in fact, boogied east, I was pressed into temporary service again until his classes were quietly reassigned to an unwitting graduate student from Kansas.

TWO

'Twas First to Beer-Drinkin'

IT OCCURS TO ME THAT THE CAREFUL reader just might conclude I was making unseemly sport of a former English Department chairman of a major Big Eight University when I told how he'd asked me whether it was okay to serve a candidate for the position of Professor of Afro-American Literature hog-head cheese and watermelon. And since the same conclusion might be reached by him and his lawyer, I figure I ought to make things right by telling you a little more about my old boss—The Chair (as we liked to call him).

The Chair was a Harvard- and Stanford-educated native New Yorker whose father had once been a respected editor at an important national magazine that you probably have somewhere in your house right now because your old maid aunt sends you a Christmas subscription every year. The Chair had somehow managed to distance himself from his conservative upbringing and became one of Norman's—if not, indeed, *America's*—truly good ol' boys. It's important to add, however, that the man was then and still is, as far as I'm able to determine, bizarre . . . a *lot* bizarre. I mean, what else am I to say about a man who once confided to me that looking at the little glass door on a microwave oven while it was turned on would cause your eyeballs to stick to the back of your glasses?

If you met The Chair in an academic setting or even, say,

strolling through a suburban shopping mall, you'd probably consider him to be a normal enough individual. But you would be wrong. For one thing, he's never deluded himself into thinking he's an adult.

I remember the first time I saw The Chair off campus. It was just about a month after my arrival at the University of Oklahoma and I was at the annual Chili Cook-Off held, appropriately enough, at a place where outlaws were said to have hidden out called Hole-in-the-Wall, Oklahoma—down by the Texas border. If memory serves, it was one of those ungodly hot August Oklahoma days with the wind blowing about a hundred and twelve miles an hour. I'd gone down to the cook-off with my friend and fellow faculty person David Mair and a couple of reasonably presentable graduate students to whom we'd taken a fancy. We had two cases of cold beer in styrofoam coolers and a couple of plastic lawn chairs. We paid three dollars to park our car in a cow pasture and then walked on down and found a place as much out of the wind as possible and set up to watch the show.

Now, in case you've never been to a big chili cook-off—or at least not to one down at Hole-in-the-Wall—you might be interested to learn that the competing chili cookers traditionally arrange their "booths" in a big oval around a patch of pasture about the size of a football field. (Incidentally, most things in Oklahoma are measured in terms of football fields—or oil derricks.) Also traditional is the way in which the spectators/chili tasters/beer drinkers who are able to walk—and that number decreases dramatically as the day progresses—stay in continuous motion around the sidelines. It always reminds me of the goings on around the midway at a state fair except it's quite a bit sleazier at a cook-off—there being a generally higher class of people who hang out around state fair midways.

The male participants in this circling menagerie dress up mostly in raggedy cut-off Levis and rubber beach thongs and wear T-shirts that proclaim things like: "I Got Crabs at Dirty Nellie's" or "I Got Scrod on Cape Cod." The women wear similar get-ups except their cut-offs are usually shorter and raggedier and a lot of times they look to be practicing up for the wet T-Shirt Contest scheduled for later on in the festivities. (The Wet T-Shirt Contest is usually staged as the big finale, coming at the end of the other events—The Moseyin' Contest and The Ugly Foot Competition being two of my personal favorites.)

Anyway, David and I were sitting there minding our own business, enjoying the parade and sipping on longneck Buds, when a short, graying man who looked as though he'd just stuck one of his mom's bobbi-pins in an electrical outlet (either that or had his hair cut down at the barber college with a weed-eater) stumbled past our place. He was wearing a dusty pair of black rugby shorts. No shoes . . . no shirt . . . nothing else.

David startled me by yelling, "Hey, you! Come on over and have a cold beer!"

I figured maybe the sun was getting to my friend—that surely he wasn't inviting the whole crowd over to share our precious beer! And he certainly couldn't be talking to the gray-haired guy in the dirty shorts. I mean *really*!

But sure enough, the fellow turned slowly and, although his eyes seemed unable to focus clearly, made his way through the crowd and over to where we were sitting. He leaned over and squinted into my face. A look of what I took to be vague recognition passed momentarily across his face. I saw then that a good deal of red Oklahoma dirt and several medium-sized clods were stuck to his back and shoulders from where, I later learned, he'd been recently sleeping under some farmer's flat-bed truck.

"Hey, Chris, you ol' sumbitch," he laughed. "Get a job!"

He hugged my neck. "Gimme a cold beer and then point me the way to the head . . ."

(For the first two years I was at OU, The Chair steadfastly confused me with my brother, Chris—never mind that my younger sibling and I have different fathers and look nothing alike; that what little hair Chris has left is blond while my shaggy mane is mostly gray; or that Chris is downright skinny and stands over six-four while I have to stand up uncomfortably straight in order to push my two-hundred-pound self to six feet even.)

Anyway, before I could reply, the guy reached one of his hands into the nearest cooler and the other into his rugby shorts. Suffice it to say he pulled out a longneck in each hand.

Now, lest you think my old boss entirely without couth, I should add that out of deference to any prudish or otherwise overly sensitive ladies who might be in the vicinity, he turned his back to the parade of gawkers passing by and, apparently feeling well-hidden, began to relieve himself on the spot.

How, you may rightly wonder, did a highly educated and respected member of the academic community manage to fall from the ivy-covered towers of Cambridge and Palo Alto to the heat and dust of a Hole-in-the-Wall cook-off? Well, if you *must* know, and since it's bound to come out anyway, I'll go ahead and reveal that at the time The Chair was a rugby player. In fact, a lot of people more up on the game than I have suggested that—though still only in his forties—he was one of the world's oldest living rugby players. (Which may account for why the rugby pitch—it's a *pitch,* not a field—at the University of Oklahoma is officially named after the man. I'm not kidding either—there's a professionally hand-painted sign, with good spelling and everything.)

So there you have it . . . the chairman of the English Department of a major university had traveled to a chili cook-off in the company of a rugby team. I subsequently learned that the man went a lot of places with the rugby team. And although I don't have any solid evidence that he ever did hard time in jail on account of that association, I've never heard him come right out and deny it, either.

It occurs to me that the more genteel reader may not be aware of the fact that rugby players have a long-standing tradition—both in this country and abroad—of being what you might call "Animals." As a group, rugby players are usually much crippled, maimed, scarred, and beat up; they are usually unemployed. Of course I doubt seriously that anybody with a regular nine-to-five job could manage the time off required to travel the great distances it takes to locate another group of like-minded rowdies and then get up a rugby match or a party. Come to think of it, I guess all the other rugby players that I've ever known personally have been out of work. Either that or they've been lawyers. (I confess I find curious the unlikely attraction of this blood sport to individuals who read the law—a pantywaist occupation I've always associated with politicians and other shysters.)

I suppose it might surprise you to learn that rugby players almost always have names like Idaho Joe, or The Reverend, or Tarzan, or Death Wish, or—and this is my personal favorite—The Evil Doctor Dick-Face. I do not believe that these are nicknames, you understand; rather they're names given to these guys by their mothers at birth. You might like to know too, that the average rugby player in training can—and regularly does—consume more draft beer in a single sitting than an entire crew of rowdy offshore oil rig workers. What's more, I've often watched rugby players down these great amounts of beer while at the same time consuming brain-numbing amounts of hard liquor and a wide variety of controlled-substance mood elevators.

I suppose all this rugby-related business must sound kind of immoral and decadent—and indeed, it is. It's just that I think you should know how far removed I was from the Red-blooded All-American Cowboy-like way of life that the reader who's attended thus far expects I'm moving toward.

THREE

Adios to All That Concrete

I REMAINED AT THE UNIVERSITY OF OKLA-
homa for four years. I suspect I would be there still—so much
did I enjoy my stay—except that the oil money dried up both
suddenly and unexpectedly. The big shots subsequently determined that they could do without about a dozen English teachers, several nuclear physicists, and a couple of cafeteria busboys.
(Naturally, the entire football coaching staff was kept on and
the recruiting fund was doubled.)

I do not mean to imply that I was turned out overnight or
without warning. I knew going into my fourth year it was to
be my last. So, during that time I half-heartedly tried to find
another teaching position. The thing is, I really did *like* it there
in Norman; I doubted I would elsewhere find as crazy a bunch
of good folks in as laid back an academic community at any
other college that might be desperate enough to offer me em-
ployment. If America has produced too much of anything other
than political assassins, surely it is teachers with Liberal Arts degrees.

I toyed briefly with the idea of finding some kind of honest
work locally and staying on in Norman. But I didn't want to
become one of those college town hangers-on that I'd always
made such sport of. You know the type: The aging victim of
LSD flashbacks who practices poor personal hygiene. The

17

freeze-dried hippie who haunts the local coffee shops and hangs around the library—showing up at rallies organized by the Young Republicans to stand in the back and shout old SDS slogans. Who continues to be invited—for a while, anyway—to faculty parties. Who holds down piddling part-time jobs so that he can keep on writing his *On the Road*–like coming-of-age novel, or his rambling, unintelligible epic poem in the manner of the *Faerie Queene*. Just a real academic Sad Sack.

Still, I hung around Norman after classes were over that last summer. I'd taken to running with a pretty loud and playful band of highly literate, semi-serious drinkers, and we whiled away the hot Oklahoma afternoons engaged in sporting events with fairly loose rules. Which is to say, contests in which league officials were not likely to come around demanding that we submit to urine tests. Pool and softball, horseshoes and the like. Our nights we spent hanging out in the air-conditioned stickiness of kicker bars across the county line like Jimmy Lee's Boogie Hill Club, or (just to prove how liberal we were) sleazy downtown Norman Indian bars like Bill & Dee's. We'd swill pitchers of beer and shoot pool or dance the Texas two-step with strangers until a fight broke out or we found ourselves no longer able to speak complete sentences in our native tongue.

As September approached and it became increasingly clear that the fall semester could—indeed, *would*—proceed without me, I packed up some books, cleaned out my office, gave Rita, the Department secretary, a kiss on the lips and my forwarding address: General Delivery, Puerto de Luna, New Mexico.

I thought I was going off to write and meditate. Certainly it was not a part of my plan to become a one-man ranch crew struggling with mean bulls, goosey cows, little dogies, and rusted barbed wire. Neither had I pictured myself busting through ice and snow to scatter feed and hay for a herd of singularly stupid and bawling cattle. Nor was I in the mood for romantic entanglements, having been much crippled and scarred in earlier wars of the heart. But one never knows. . . .

FOUR

Home on the Range . . .
(More or Less)

I DIDN'T CHOOSE TO LIVE IN PUERTO DE
Luna for any romantic reasons. Rather I chose to live there because my friend A. T. Austin owns a three-hundred-and-some-
odd-acre place on the Pecos River where he breeds Thoroughbred racehorses. About a quarter of a mile from his house is an
old three-room adobe in which some previous owner used to
keep wetbacks, and which happened to be empty that fall.
A. T. offered to let me stay in the little house rent-free, and that
was enough to inspire my immigration from Norman.

The water there is bad. Soap won't lather; clothes turn gray
with washing; a hot water heater is good for only a couple of
years before rusting and clogging; and pipes—like aging arteries—build up scaley deposits until one day they shut down
completely. I hauled water in plastic gallon milk jugs for drinking and cooking. It was a pain in the ass.

But then, bald eagles nest in the red rock cliffs across the
river from the house; porcupines and beavers roam the irriga-
tion ditches. I watched deer pass within fifty feet of my front
door most mornings. And there were the two old geldings—
not good for much now, but who long ago earned their keep
on racetracks and so were allowed the run of the place. They
wandered about, at will and inseparable, startling me or an oc-

19

casional visitor from time to time by peering in the bathroom window.

Puerto de Luna is about ten miles south of Santa Rosa, New Mexico. You may have passed through Santa Rosa without really noticing—it's a fairly nondescript place where travelers occasionally stop en route to someplace else. It's on Interstate 40, midway between Tucumcari and Clines Corners. Santa Rosa is one of those Interstate towns made up mostly of motels and gas station-cafe combinations with flashing red and green neon signs that advertise—alternately—GAS . . . EAT . . . GAS . . . EAT.

Don't get me wrong, Santa Rosa is not without its attractions. Besides a very deep and very clear pool of spring water—Blue Hole, it's called—in which scuba enthusiasts from all over come to dive and occasionally to drown, and one of the world's shortest rivers, there's a Dairy Queen and next door to that a Holiday Inn with a lounge featuring live entertainment three or four nights a week.

The featured entertainer at the Holiday Inn is more often than not a one-man band whose guitar is plugged into some kind of Japanese computerized contraption that makes it sound as though he's backed up by a concert hall full of pianos and drums and flutes and oboes and harmonicas. And who, although he's obviously had little formal musical training, is blessed with a talent for making his voice sound like Conway Twitty or Little Jimmie Dickens or whoever happens to be at the top of the C&W charts that week. Of course, the lounge is decorated in your typical motel-plastic Baja California style with paintings of Day-glo bullfighters on black velvet; and red brandy snifter candle holders wrapped in fishnet are on all the tables. On Friday nights westbound truckers sporting 1950s-style ducktail hair-dos, long wallets sticking from their hip pockets and attached to their belts by what I've always taken to be choke chains, sit and drink longneck Buds and stare out from under their amphetamine-swollen eyelids across the room at heavily made-up ladies who chain smoke Virginia Slims 100s and chew gum while they sip fluffy pink frozen fruit and Ron

Rico rum drinks through little red cocktail straws; I am talking semi-serious romance here. The women are called Wanda and Trudi and Earline; they work at the Truckstops of America or the Stuckeys out on the Interstate because they weren't lucky or talented enough to graduate from Beautician's College. They all have ill-mannered children at home in the trailer park, but their husbands are little more than dim memories.

Puerto de Luna, on the other hand, is more off the beaten path. It boasts no motel, no gas station, no cafe . . . not so much as a 7-11 or a Toot-N-Tote. It is, rather, a quiet little village of mud and stone. Situated on the banks of the Pecos River, Puerto de Luna is the place where Francisco Vásquez de Coronado is reported to have crossed that river in 1541. More importantly, perhaps, it's where the outlaw Billy the Kid is supposed to have spent his final Christmas Eve in the company of a local Mexican woman of questionable virtue—locked in heavenly transport, so they say.

For the most part, I enjoyed the life I lived in Puerto de Luna. It was a solitary life—lonely at times. Accustomed as I was to the university community and the raucousness of what living there entailed, I gradually learned to cope with the quiet. It complimented what I had come to refer to as "the life of the mind."

I read a lot. I joined the three major book clubs and never went to Santa Fe or Albuquerque or anyplace else with a bookstore but what I brought home a half-dozen volumes. With the aid of some aluminum foil from a TV dinner and wire coat hangers, I was finally able to situate my small black-and-white television set in a position near a kitchen window where it would occasionally pick up a station from Albuquerque. On clear evenings I could sometimes make out a shadowy Dan Rather or, with luck, ghostly flickers of "Late Night with David Letterman." Still, I found myself longing for more companionship in odd moments than my television set provided.

Then one of A. T.'s dogs had a litter of pups—the result of a planned coupling with a male of the same breed, I might add, and not merely one of your chance encounters. When Suzie had

Lefty and Ron

her pups, I put in for the only male—who happened also to be
the runt of the bunch. I brought him down to my house when
he was about eight weeks old.

Lefty is a Queensland Blue Heeler. For you unfortunate city-
dwellers, a Blue Heeler is a breed of working cow dog. His
coarse coat of mixed black and white hair makes Lefty appear
to be blue—I don't mean to say that he looks *depressed,* you understand, but rather that he is an attractive shade of the *color*
blue. And the fact that the breed just naturally drives livestock
by snapping at their lower legs and feet accounts, I suppose, for
the term "heeler."

We became fast friends. I don't know if it's insecurity or loy-
alty or what, but Lefty always seems to have to be touching
me. If he's in the house and I'm sitting and reading or whatever, he will lie on my foot. Or he'll sometimes sit for long periods of time with his head on my lap. He walks right at my
heel when we're afoot—another reason he's called a heeler?—
and if I'm horseback, he'll walk in the horse's shadow. If I stand
still for more than a minute, he'll sit on my boot. As I write
this, Lefty is outside the window that my desk faces, curled up
pretending to be asleep . . . his back against the wall of the
house as close to the sound of my clacking typewriter as he can
manage.

When he was about four months old, Lefty went with me on
a long road trip. Together we went to Oklahoma to visit friends
in Norman; to Alabama to see my sister and to meet my
daughter on spring break from college; and then on to Houston
to visit my outlaw friend, rodeo-clown-turned-lawyer Kirk
Purcell. We made the trip in my Toyota pickup. Except when it
rained, Lefty rode in the back. He preferred the back. I don't
know why, it just seemed like he was convinced he wasn't supposed to be up front in the cab. I believe he thought it was like
being on the furniture in the house . . . something for which
he'd been scolded on more than one occasion.

If Lefty and I hadn't been close friends before that trip, we
sure would have been by the time it was over. We never stayed
in one place very long during a three-week trek that took us

This steer is just about to get his nose nipped by a little cow dog who figures he's got no business stickin' it in his truck

across New Mexico, Texas, Oklahoma, Arkansas, Tennessee, Mississippi, Alabama, and Louisiana. Lefty learned to stay with the truck: he by god *wasn't* going to get left behind.

I suspect, too, that he would have eventually come to love riding in what came to be *his* truck, anyway, but that trip clinched it for him. He'll leave a T-bone steak for a ride in his truck—I've seen him do it. If the engine's running, he won't get down out of the truck unless I holler at him to do so (and then he'll jump back in if he thinks I'm not looking). The ultimate joy for Lefty—next to working cattle, which he *lives* for—is to ride down a dirt road after a rain and, dashing madly from one side of the truck to the other, snap at the water that splashes up from the tires hitting puddles. He used to like to snap at bushes and tree branches when we passed close and they were within striking distance—until the time he snapped at a cactus plant. Lefty is *not* one of your slow learners.

He considers it his duty to guard his truck against inquisitive horses and cows that have the nerve to stick their noses where they don't have any business—in the bed of his truck!

And jumping. Lefty can jump from a flat-footed stance to a height of five or six feet straight up. I know he can jump that high because I built a pen with a five-foot fence to keep him in when he started following his truck when he was supposed to stay at home. He gets so excited when he sees me coming down the drive and knows that I'm going to let him out of "jail" that he leaps straight up to a height considerably greater than the top of the fence. He could, with but a slight lateral movement, easily escape from his pen.

But like I say, life on the banks of the Pecos River was, for the most part, solitary and pretty much kicked back. I read a lot and I wrote a little. It was just me and Lefty.

Then I met Miss Elaine.

FIVE

Romance in the Branding Pens

I CHANCED TO MEET ELAINE BREECE STRIB-
ling because she had recently bought a Quarter Horse mare that
was in foal and had brought her over to A. T.'s place so that
when Josie had her baby, she could be bred back to one of the
stallions that A. T. was standing. Elaine used to visit Josie every
couple of days. After I'd seen her a time or two, I promised
each of A. T.'s little girls—Navata and Lanita—a quarter if
they'd call me on the phone whenever she showed up. Only
later did I discover that Lanita, who considered the whole thing
quite romantic, would giggle and announce to Elaine that she
had to go call Ron and tell him "You know who" was there.
All that time I figured Elaine just thought it was a coincidence
that I happened past the mare pens when she was there—that,
or else I sure walked my dog a lot.

Elaine lived alone with *her* dog—a black Lab named Domino—on nine and a half square miles of cattle ranch some twenty
miles west of Santa Rosa. When I say alone, I want you to understand that she didn't have so much as a hired hand. She ran
the ranch—and managed the livestock—all by herself.

The place had originally been homesteaded by her great-
grandparents and had been in Elaine's family ever since. As near
as I could tell, Elaine was the only one left who had any real
feelings about the place—the others seemed to have very little

interest in what happened on or to the ranch. On rare occasions, friends and other folks would come to visit Elaine. One, I remember, was an out-of-state suburban housewife with two children. Her husband, as I understand it, claimed to be a "Dee-Jay" and played records at junior high school sock hops. I only saw her show up a couple of times, but when she did she'd smear herself and her children with copious amounts of sunscreen and insect repellent and make everybody don giant, wide-brimmed hats before arming her entire little band with long, pointed sticks with which to fend off cows and chickens and other dangerous rural creatures and venture out as far as the shady side of the house—there to spray water on anything that looked dry to her, be it rosebush or locoweed, lilac or mesquite. I think she liked to tell people back home that she'd been out "ranching."

There were some changes in my life—indeed, in my life-*style*—once I met Elaine. A. T. and Norma were the first to point out that I had become considerably more careful about my personal hygiene: I shaved every day rather than just occasionally, and I started wearing Levis and boots again instead of the ragged old khaki pants and sneakers without laces that I'd taken such a fancy to.

The "dating" Elaine and I did was unlike that of most courting couples. We didn't go to movies or to the theater; we didn't frequent nightclubs or go out dancing until dawn. From time to time we would get dressed up and drive over to Santa Fe—a hundred and twenty-five miles each way—for dinner at a fancy restaurant ("fancy" being the term Santa Rosa folks used to describe an eating place that didn't also sell diesel fuel), and then back to the ranch in time to sit on the couch and hold hands and watch the 10 o'clock news on her color TV. And sometimes we'd go to a calf roping in Tucumcari or the horseraces in Albuquerque. Mostly, though, we courted while rehanging gates that were falling down in her branding pens, or mending fence, or doctoring sick calves.

Naturally, I was trying to make the best impression possible, and to appear as handy around the ranch as any of the other fel-

28

lows—be they cowboys or former college English professors—who might be vying for her attentions. So when Elaine wondered if I'd give her a hand with branding a new yearling bull she'd just gotten as a replacement for the old herd sire that was getting along in years, I felt both proud she'd asked and, at the same time, filled with trepidation that I might be discovered for the pantywaist city slicker I had a feeling I really was. I swallowed hard and, with all the enthusiasm I could muster, said "Sure!" or "Yup" or something equally appropriate.

We arranged that I would show up at her place around mid-morning on the day we were going to perform the deed. Elaine promised to fix a gourmet lunch in return for my labor; having seen inside the icebox at my house, she rightly figured I'd brand everything in the county for something decent to eat that hadn't been frozen in tinfoil.

She had the bull penned up when I arrived, and was building a fire to heat the branding irons. Elaine had told me that this new bull of hers was a yearling, and I had naturally assumed that meant he was a little calf-like animal. *Wrong* . . . The black son-of-a-bitch must of weighed in at eight or nine hundred pounds! I was relieved to see that he was either of the breed that is born without horns or else someone with good sense had removed them early on.

A squeeze chute, I learned that morning, is a large, sturdy contraption made from welded steel and pipe and other strong materials that, by means of a series of handles and cranks and gears and pulleys and chains and gates, is designed to hold members of the bovine species captive and immobile while human beings do to them things that they wouldn't otherwise stand for. Elaine must have figured I was a fast study, because she didn't break out the instruction manual or even speak slowly while she told me which handle to pull at what point in the capturing process, and cautioned me not to miss the bull on the first try or we'd sure enough have hell catching him again. Then she pointed to where I should stand, picked up a stick, and went back in the pen to drive him down the alley into the chute.

My knees felt all rubbery and my hands were sweating and slick as I watched this sweet young girl yelling and beating on that fire-breathing killer bull's ass while she drove him toward me.

When the animal you're aiming to catch enters the confines of the squeeze chute, it is faced with but two logical choices: to poke its head through a space designed for its head to be poked through, or to stand still. The first choice is the one you hope for. Should the animal choose to stand still, you then have to punch and beat and kick and holler until it chooses to poke its head into the head hole. Once that happens, you jerk down on a big lever that causes some gears to do something so that the beast's neck is caught in a vise-like stranglehold and you can have your way with your victim.

That's how it's supposed to happen. Subsequent experience has shown me that most cattle, not being vulnerable to reason, see a good many more than those two choices once they're inside the chute. What's more, the animal generally makes another choice: It may choose to flip over backwards, or to climb straight up the side of the chute, or to get down on its knees and refuse to budge; you can't really predict what it will do.

This bull, however, chose to do what he was supposed to do. He gently placed his head into the headstall. As though I'd done it every day of my life, I calmly reached up and pulled the proper handle, catching the animal neatly by its neck. (Looking back now, I figure that's the exact moment Elaine recognized she was in the presence of the man of her dreams.) I just barely was able to stifle my impulse to rear back, flap my arms, and shout "Ya-Hoo!," so pleased was I with my performance.

Outwardly, I tried to appear cool, as though this was all old hat to me. In truth, I was still feeling like I was ready to apply for the head wrangler's job at the King Ranch or to call up Hollywood and offer to fill the void left by John Wayne's untimely demise when Elaine laid a white-hot branding iron against the bull's right hip and he exploded in a fit of rage. All hell broke loose as the bellowing bastard tried to tear down the squeeze chute, the branding pens, and my ego. I jumped up and

Branding. (The smoke behind Elaine means the iron was hot.)

grabbed the handle and hung on with all my might. For a while I was tossed around on the end of the handle like a rag doll.

Then the bull got real still.

Elaine calmly finished branding and put in an eartag. All the while, my nearly two hundred pounds was hanging from the end of that handle . . . inadvertently choking the bull to death.

When Elaine finally got my attention and instructed me to let him go, it took me a full minute or more to figure out how to undo the ratchet-like gear that I had applied with such finality. Then, when I *did* release his head, the bull just sort of slithered down to his knees in the chute . . . out like a light. I kicked the latch so that the side of the chute swung open, and the unconscious animal flopped out into the dust.

I figured I'd blown all chances at serious romance by involuntarily murdering this woman's new bull. I knew I had to do something to salvage this disaster; I doubted seriously that Elaine would even fix me lunch now.

Luck was with both me and the bull that day, however. Even before I could leap into action and assume the proper position to administer life-saving CPR, the bull gave a giant shudder, moaned, slobbered, and struggled clumsily to his feet. He walked headlong into the side of the pickup, bellowed his rage a couple of times more, and staggered off into the pasture. But he was alive!

I should tell you that the bull has never been quite right since that day, although he's turned out to be extremely virile as a herd sire. Because of his two most obvious traits—his mental deficiency and his reputation as an insatiable lover, both at home and on neighboring ranches—television watchers around Guadalupe County have taken to calling him Retardo Montal-bull.

As I got to know Elaine I discovered that not only was she a top-notch cow rancher, she was a crackerjack photographer, as well. In fact, she used to be a newspaper photographer and had a darkroom set up in her house where she did black-and-white developing and print work. I don't know when's the last time you tried to get any black-and-white film developed or printed, but if it's been awhile, let me tell you it's *tough*. If you can find someone willing to do it, it takes twice as long and is at least three times as expensive as color prints. Now, imagine yourself in Santa Rosa, New Mexico—there's no Fox Foto . . . there's not even a drugstore! I know, it sounds unreasonable, and it is. Being a free-lance writer with editors who sometimes get up-pity and demand good quality black-and-white prints with stories, I knew a good thing when I saw one. And Miss Elaine was just about the best thing I'd seen, even without her dark-room. I may be a slow learner in a lot of areas, but in this in-stance I knew exactly what I had to do.

Now, I'm going to skip over a lot of the good stuff here, be-cause this isn't that kind of book. I'll admit, though, that I did try and revert to my old ways in that I begged and cajoled this pretty rancher-lady to just let me move in with her. But having been raised by what I figure must have been Republican church workers and being somewhat narrow-minded herself, she simply wouldn't hear of it.

Miss Elaine and I were married at the ranch one windy afternoon in the middle of May.

It wasn't your big society-type wedding. None of my family showed up, seeing as how they were spread out across the United States. And none of her family was there because . . . well, just because. In fact, the entire wedding party was made up of A. T. and Norma and their three kids (who had insisted on playing hookey from school that day so as not to miss the nuptials).

Lefty and his new partner Domino roughoused under our feet the whole time. Domino suffered then—and still does, occasionally—from gender confusion, and so attempted repeatedly to mount Lefty during the exchange of vows. I don't know, maybe it was all the romance in the air.

We were married outdoors, in front of the bunkhouse, under an old apricot tree.

The legally ordained Methodist minister, whose name A. T. got from the fellow who runs the feedstore, told us how things weren't real good in the preaching business and that he had a weekday job as a mail carrier. He wore a brown corduroy suit with a matching vest and a clip-on necktie even though the temperature was in the high eighties.

The wedding party threw Minute Rice (except for Travis— A. T.'s youngest—who got carried away and started throwing pebbles and then chunkin' rocks). Then we all went in the house and ate German chocolate cake and sipped red imitation fruit punch the kids had chosen as appropriate wedding refreshments from the Allsup's store in Santa Rosa. (I figured out later that the Allsup's probably hadn't catered all that many weddings before, which explains the German chocolate cake.)

The big wedding at Lake Ranch, May 14, 1984. From left to right: Travis, Navata, Elaine, Ron, Lanita, The Reverend Mailman, Domino, and Lefty.

Talk about your turnarounds. I'd come in the gate and down the drive with little more than my dog Lefty, a secondhand manual typewriter, and a couple of boxes of books. Now look at me: Not only did I have a beautiful new bride, but I was the head of a vast cattle empire!

Understand, Lake Ranch is not to be confused with South Fork—where J. R. and most of the other Ewings live. It is, rather, a flat, dry, hardscrabble place. It takes every drop of what little rain falls on its sparse grasses to support the seventy-odd cows at home on that range. Drooping stretches of rusting and much mended barbed wire that would be better off displayed in some aficionado's antique collection try their best to resemble fences. I lived in constant fear that professional pipe-smoking archaeologists in pith helmets and safari jackets would one day show up at our door exclaiming excitedly over their discovery of crude remnants of primitive livestock enclosures left from some ancient tribe of root gatherers. And *I* would have to be the one to tell them that all they'd discovered was a stretch of our best boundary fence.

I'm confident, too, that were the cows not all named things like Lucy and Bonnie and Startled (Startled has an unruly sprig of hair that sticks straight up between her ears) and treated and talked to like house pets, they'd have long ago walked over or through our fences. The windbreaks barely did break wind and those structures we called barns whenever city slickers were within earshot tilted and swayed dangerously in even the slightest breeze. As for corrals and holding pens . . . well, like I said, the livestock really did *like* it there.

I never met Elaine's grandfather. Before his death in 1980, my bride and he had been extremely close. It's clear to me that the very reason Elaine chose to live on the ranch in the first place, and to try and make a go of keeping the place together as a working cattle ranch, in spite of the real and imagined hardships attendant to a single woman's undertaking such a chore, was because of her close relationship with the old man. She had grown up watching George Bibb work the ranch. Everything she knew about ranching and the cattle business—and it was, and is, a considerable amount—came from her grandfather. She didn't know any other way. So what happens? Here I came along, the new kid who admittedly wasn't famous for being a cow puncher, and right away I started trying to make "improvements."

Take the area immediately around the house—the "headquarters," as we big-time ranchers like to call it. Junk had been accumulating there for three-quarters of a century. I'm convinced that not once in all the time before I arrived on the scene had a single item been removed from the property as trash. Instead, anything for which no reasonable use was immediately obvious

35

had been carried, thrown, dragged, or coaxed onto one of several large piles, just in case it might come in handy for something or become a collector's item during the next forty or fifty years. Becoming a future collector's item did *not* mean that the semi-rare object in question should be sold or turned over to a museum; no, it should remain on the pile and be pointed out and bragged on to visitors. In fairness, I should tell you that the frequency, velocity, and constancy of the prevailing winds sweeping across Lake Ranch were such that untethered objects weighing less than six or seven pounds did not accumulate, and so were not a problem.

Like wire.

I'll wager there was enough rusting barbed and baling wire clumped and scattered around the ranch that compasses and other magnetic navigational devices located within a hundred miles in any direction were rendered unreliable if not inoperable. Perhaps New Mexico is far enough removed from any major body of water that merchant ships were seldom affected; however, I've personally observed commercial airliners passing over Guadalupe County suddenly swerve off course. You get the notion: there was wire everywhere.

And old tires. The first day I drove onto the ranch I noticed there were enough old tires scattered around to decorate the roof of every trailer house in Tucumcari. And baling twine. And scrap iron. And tin. And things I can't name since I've no idea what they were. But then I guess black widows and rattlesnakes need a place to hang out, same as everybody else.

When I announced to Elaine that I'd broken with her family's long-standing tradition and inquired at the feedstore for directions to the town dump, I swear I think she figured I wanted to go get some *more* junk; she seemed genuinely pleased to see I was fitting in so well. But I heaped the bed of the pickup and the stock trailer to overflowing on many occasions, and hauled away tons of precious junk. Still, it was always hard to see where I'd ever made much of a dent.

And none of this takes into account the stuff I wanted to haul off but, in the interests of marital harmony, didn't. Crap like

A young George Bibb (probably taken about 1910)

leaky boats and flat-tired bicycles and broken-down box springs and other items appropriate to Tobacco Road that my in-laws stored there because their cities had enough sense to pass ordinances prohibiting such clutter. It's enough to induce deep depression in one whose blood isn't inherited from Grandpa Bibb.

When there was something to be done, I could usually count on a lecture about how Grandpa would have done it. Don't get me wrong: I respect my elders, the wisdom of age and experience and so forth. It's just that there's some things that I know better than. I know in my heart a big wad of slobbery chewing tobacco is *not* the best medicine for a wire cut on a horse's leg.

37

And burned motor oil drained from the crankcase of a John Deere is *not* the best thing in the world with which to paint board fences—nor is it a good hoof dressing for your saddle horse. And I don't agree that the best way to keep from getting stuck on a muddy pasture road is to grab ahold of the steering wheel with both hands and mash down on the accelerator pedal with all your might; one look at the pickup truck Elaine inherited with the ranch, or at what's left of the gates between the pastures around the place, will convince anyone not named Bibb that the Mario Andretti Mud Method can't possibly work.

Elaine's grandfather was a good man, a fine and knowledgeable rancher. He put the better part of his life into that place, and so it stands to reason that his ghost walks strong and tall. To folks around Santa Rosa, it is the "George Bibb Place"; Elaine and her tenderfoot new husband merely worked it for a while. I suspect it will always be that way; perhaps that's as it should be. I feel certain I would have liked George Bibb. I like to think we'd have been friends, had we been able to see one another over the junkpile.

Like the livestock, I really liked it there. Once I'd gotten pretty well settled in, I subscribed to the *Livestock Weekly* out of San Angelo, Texas, and started keeping up with feeder cattle prices and beef futures trading at the Chicago Mercantile Exchange. I wrote long letters to old friends back east in Oklahoma, inviting them to come help with roundups and cattle drives.

Yessir, I figured I was gonna do just fine as a big-time rancher in the cattle bidness.

SIX

I See by My Get-Up
That I Am a Cowboy

WITHIN A WEEK OF THE WEDDING, LEFTY
killed all thirteen of Elaine's laying hens.

It was tense for awhile, but I managed to convince my new
bride that the cholesterol in eggs was bad for our arteries and
that, besides, Domino *had* to have helped out with the slaughter
or at the very least have shown the new pup where the chickens
hung out.

I reminded her, too, that I was pretty handy to have around.
That I had propped up some fence in a couple of places and had
even, on at least one occasion, made Leo Camarillo look like a
rank amateur with my natural talent for lassoing a fast-moving
calf from the bed of a wildly bouncing pickup. Not for time or
prize money like Camarillo does it, you understand, but rather
so that I could leap upon the scared and bawling calf and poke
jumbo scour boluses down its throat.

We'd only been married about two weeks when Elaine announced that the honeymoon was over and that we had to
brand, ear-tag, dehorn, emasculate, spray, and/or dip everything bovine on the place.

What with Lefty being a registered, card-carrying cow dog, I
figured he would know what to do, and maybe even redeem
himself for the henhouse massacre. I hoped so, anyway; because
while it's true I'd wrangled a right fair number of horses in my

39

day, the closest I'd ever come to an honest-to-goodness cattle roundup and branding—not counting the Retardo Montalbull Incident, which I hoped Elaine had erased from her memory—had been watching Hollywood waddies do it up on the silver screen or on the electric television set. Of course, Elaine and the couple of neighbors who were coming over to help out had a good deal of cow experience among them. And my wife said things couldn't possibly turn out as bad as last year, when she'd lost three good calves to complications from castration and de-horning. Okay, so I *know* she just told me that to boost my confidence. How was she to know it had never even occurred to me that anything we were setting out to do might prove fatal?

The day before the branding I got myself some good eight-dollar leather gloves down at the feedstore, and tried to scuff up my shiny new Tony Lama boots so as not to look too much the greenhorn. I even spent an hour before supper practicing jerking on the handles of the squeeze chute and squirting oil on all the moving parts.

Later that evening, Elaine confided that when the light hit me just right, I looked a lot like Paul Newman in *Hud*. That night I dreamed I was being presented with a trophy buckle as big as a dozer blade for having won the All Around title at the National Finals Rodeo.

Yessir, I was ready.

Things didn't start off exactly like I'd pictured they would. The old timer from Albuquerque who was bringing the calf cradle—a device that not only squeezes and holds the calf, but allows its tormentors to swing the bawling critter up on its side so they can perform all manner of unspeakable acts upon its frightened self—showed up before I'd gotten my Levis on, or had my first sip of coffee. Even though we hadn't met, he'd evidently felt sorry for Elaine and had promised to teach her new husband how to castrate the bull calves. He looked at my longish hair and new boots, shook his head and grunted that maybe he'd got the wrong day, what with not having seen any cattle in the branding pens when he drove in.

I mumbled back some lie about a faulty alarm clock and hurried off to catch and saddle Moonshine and Rumshop, our two old borrowed geldings who, I prayed, had enough sense between them to bring in cows. Moonshine packs camp supplies once a year for his elk-hunter owner, and Rumshop retired from a singularly unspectacular career on the racetrack a good many years ago.

I'm relieved to report that the horses did just fine.

And I was proud of Lefty, too. He stayed right with Rumshop and me and even acted halfway smart when a goosey bull calf we call Lawrence—for you literary types, we also have a heifer we call Frieda and one named Brett—bolted a time or two and tried to turn back.

Domino, on the other hand, took the opportunity of being out in the big pasture to wander off in search of horny toads— creatures he considers to be highly dangerous to both human beings and domesticated animals. When he discovers a horny toad, he'll stand over it, barking madly, until someone comes to praise his great courage. I have personally observed Domino stop and look casually for a moment at a five-foot rattlesnake, yawn, and then amble off in his never-ending search for the dreaded horny toad.

By the time Elaine and I had rounded up our victims, A. T. had arrived from his place in Puerto de Luna.

About then the wind started to blow. And a good bit of eastern New Mexico was in the air, seeing as how the only rain we'd had for two months had measured a paltry tenth of an inch in the rain gauge down by the windmill—and that included a dead miller moth in the bottom of the gauge.

Lefty did a fine job in his initial foray into the world of the working cow dog, and I was quite proud of him. That is, until we got to the part where we were supposed to separate the mother cows from their calves. It was right in there somewhere that Lefty's day started to go sour.

Domino is very proud of this bone he's found out in the pasture.

After having been walked on and kicked a time or two by wise old mother cows, Lefty deduced that maybe he was approaching his work from the wrong end; keep in mind he was just a pup and had never had any formal training. Anyway, he determined he might be better off if he'd drive the cows from the front—snapping at their noses instead of their heels. This approach caused great concern among all those present. The one who seemed the most startled by the change in tactics was Rumshop. When he saw Lefty leap high in the air and snap at Elaine's stirrup in a moment of over-zealousness, he must have thought the dog had contracted rabies and might be fixing to attack the horses as soon as he'd done in all the humans. Anyway, at that point Rumshop either kicked or stepped on Lefty's leg, effectively retiring him from further duty.

Humbled and humiliated, reduced to the role of onlooker, my little cow dog spent the rest of the day parked in the shade of the loading chute.

Once the cattle had been penned and separated, it became clear that I could no longer avoid making my cowhand debut. Elaine assigned me to operate the squeeze chute—I'd already proven myself on that contraption, I guess—and to run the calf cradle.

Our squeeze chute was a rusted, baling-wire-mended, medieval-looking device that I suspect had held countless numbers of cattle over the years as they were being poked and jabbed and burned. The best I can report is that I finished the day with all my fingers and toes and the same number of teeth with which I started; subsequent experience persuades me that that fact is, indeed, remarkable. I only came close to killing one animal all day, and that was early on when I again choked down an animal in the chute; this one, a heifer, recovered fully within a minute or two, and staggered off to join the rest of the herd. At least as long as we owned her she showed no sign of the kind of permanent brain damage that the bull Retardo suffered.

Miss Elaine handled the branding irons in a manner to cause John Wayne and other working cowboys to hide their faces in

Ron and A. T. castrating a bull calf. (Domino likes to eat what the fellows are removing.)

shame and to mutter about smart-assed womenfolk who ought to stay home and take care of children. A. T. vaccinated, ear-tagged, and squirted tick dope. Leo—the early bird from Albuquerque—dehorned and castrated. Some woman Elaine knew armed herself with a stick and wandered around watering cactus, while her husband drank beer and tried to avoid getting cowshit on his brand new jogging shoes.

I said that Leo castrated—actually, he only cut the first two bull calves to show me how it was done. No rubber bands or bloodless emasculators on *this* ranch. No *sir*. We worked quickly and cleanly on Lake Ranch: with a sharp pocket knife. While they might just as soon have been left "entire," all the new little steers survived the ordeal just fine and seemed no worse for the

Lefty, under his truck

insult. That's what Elaine assured me, anyway, when she noticed me looking a shade pale.

We finished all our dirty work by midafternoon. Except for Lefty's disgrace and the blowing dirt, things had gone smoothly enough. After we'd fed the crew and everyone had headed home, I went out to reward Rumshop and Moonshine with an extra flake of alfalfa for not having embarrassed me in front of neighbors. Lefty seemed to be feeling a little better, and even managed to scramble into the bed of the pickup on his three good legs.

After visiting with the horses a few minutes, I climbed in the truck to head back up to the house. I guess Lefty must have slipped or something. I don't really know. But as I pulled away, I heard a high-pitched yelp and felt a bump as a rear wheel passed over my already battered little cow dog.

I was heartsick. By the time I got out of the truck and found

45

him, Lefty had crawled up under a cedar and was lying in the shade. Blood was coming from his mouth and bubbling from his nostrils with an awful gurgling noise. His breathing was quick and shallow.

I anguished over whether or not to shoot him then and there and end his misery, or to try and rush him to the nearest vet over seventy miles distant. I couldn't bring myself to shoot him, and I reasoned that it was too late in the day to find the veterinarian at the clinic.

The next morning I was prepared for the worst. I expected to find Lefty dead or, worse yet, dying. But there he was, waiting beside his truck to go on our morning rounds as usual . . . roughousing with his pal Domino. That little dog is one tough hombre . . . believe it!

SEVEN

Farrier (n.), "a man who shoes horses"

OKAY, YOU'RE SAYING TO YOURSELF, here's this smart-assed unemployed school teacher trying to pass himself off to the poor innocent rancher lady as some kind of wrangler. Now if that doesn't sound fishy, I don't know what does. I told you early on that I used to work with horses, but I guess I didn't mention that I started out working with horses as a farrier.

Let's get one thing straight here. If you aim to use the word *farrier* when addressing a man who claims to be one—especially if he's tired or cranky, and he usually is—do not smile, or chortle, or giggle, or snicker, or in any way indicate that you find that term amusing. Farriers—especially cranky farriers—tend to be very bad actors. Which is to say most of the ones I've come across are prone to cuss and drink hard liquor and just generally act loud and nasty in mixed company, and then casually stomp a mudhole in the backside of anyone who might question his good judgment in having done so.

It should come as no surprise to learn of this sordid character trait in a person who draws slave wages for picking up a twelve-hundred-pound animal's leg and nailing—yes, *nailing!*— a piece of iron to the bottom of its foot. Face it—that sumbitch has just nearly *got* to be mean!

I just don't count myself among the mean. That fact in itself is all that's required to disqualify me from ever working as a farrier. On top of that, though, I've never especially cared for strenuous physical activities that produce sweat, and I generally try to avoid participating (or stepping) in things that'll get me dirty. I don't know about you, but I've always hated having something smelly stuck to the bottom of my shoe. And I've never been one of those clever people who can accurately hit a nail with a hammer—at least not with any consistency. I am not, you might say, into macho stuff.

On the other hand, I've always had a real hang-up when it comes to paying cash money to somebody to do for me what I figure I can just as well do for myself for free, like changing the oil in my truck, or fixing a leaky faucet. There's something about paying some dude an extra eight or ten cents a gallon just to hold a spigot while gasoline pumps into my tank that somehow doesn't seem right. I guess you could call me cheap—a lot of people have.

Anyway, you can imagine my feelings when I discovered that I had to wait sometimes as long as six weeks to get the local horseshoer to come out to my place and spend thirty minutes putting a new pair of shoes on my daughter's pet mare and then charge me twenty-five dollars to do so. Why, the way I saw it (then) was that that guy was making fifty dollars an hour—and he was booked up six weeks in advance!

I decided to apply to horseshoer's school.

Now, I don't want to mislead you here . . . the term *apply* naturally carries with it the connotation of an acceptance. In fact, I discovered that in order to be accepted to horseshoer's school the prospective scholar need only present a check or postal money order in the amount of the required tuition. Unless your check is returned for insufficient funds, you've taken your first step toward mastering the skills necessary to take up the lucrative career of the Professional Farrier.

There were several schools to consider—as I recall I was able to choose from a list of over twenty. The instruction was characteristically proclaimed by each to be the best of its kind. The courses ranged from two to twelve weeks and covered such diverse subjects as Conformation & Anatomy, Physiology of the Foot, Analysis of Gaits, and Customer Relations, as well as the techniques of shoeing the animals. The four-color brochure for one school in Oklahoma showed pictures of smiling students happily whittling away at the feet of not only horses, but of goats, cows, and a Brahma bull as well!

Tuition for the various schools ranged anywhere from a couple of hundred dollars to over a thousand at Oklahoma Farrier's College. (But then, OFC *did* represent itself to be an institution of higher learning, and the owner of this "college" bragged about how they had a display of his fancy hand-made horseshoes at the Cowboy Hall of Fame over in Oklahoma City—both of which would tend to make a place more expensive, I suppose.)

Actually, the cost of the school was not important. Or at least so said the schools. The satisfaction that came with knowing that "you, as a graduate of the leading Farrier's College in the Nation, can earn upwards of $30,000 a year in an enjoyable profession," should make even the most outrageous tuition seem miniscule.

"To hell with graduate school," I thought. Why not become a horseshoer and earn big bucks in an enjoyable profession. So, outfitting myself with several pairs of stiff new bootcut Levis, a half-dozen flowerdy western shirts with mother-of-pearl snaps that I got on sale at K-Mart, a straw hat, and a new pair of Acme cowboy boots, I climbed into my Japanese pickup truck and drove off to spend just three more weeks in school. *This* time, by god, I was going to learn to do something practical—something that would make me a wealthy man.

The Farrier Science Course at New Mexico State University was a three-week session that cost $175. The head farrier instructor at NMSU was, and I'll wager still is, M. I. "Ras" Rasmussen, a native of some Scandinavian country who for reasons of dialect or speech impediment—I was never able to ascertain which—was unable to pronounce his R's. He introduced himself, Elmer Fudd–like, as "*Wass Wassmussen.*"

The course was comparatively inexpensive; it was widely cir-

Josie and Rumshop

culated (by Wass) that Wass was the best damned horseshoer to be found anywhere; and because it was affiliated with a real university and not merely a trade school, the course carried with it a hint of respectability—important to one having spent the better part of his life attending half the colleges in the Northern Hemisphere. At the not-so-tender age of thirty-one, I had missed but three years of being continuously enrolled in school since kindergarten—and that only because I'd heard that "The Marine Corps Builds Men" and foolishly decided to see just how it was they accomplished that wondrous feat. Anyway, because I'd long ago heeded the advice of my teachers and developed good study habits, I was able to breeze through the theory portion of the farrier course with a record-setting score of 99 percent. The field work—the actual shoeing of the horse—was another matter.

FARRIER (N.), "A MAN WHO SHOES HORSES"

It may surprise you to learn that the average farrier can shoe a horse in minus-15-degree cold dressed casually in jockey shorts and T-shirt and still feel flushed from the heat—the work is *that* hard. But when the temperature is 102 in the shade . . . well, I can report that my research shows a horseshoer can actually sweat six to eight quart jars of Gatorade out of his system before it reaches his tonsils, not to mention his kidneys.

And of course the horse is hot, too. And there's about two-thousand and sixty-seven flies buzzing around due to all the horseshit in the immediate vicinity. And likely as not, the horse is pissed off at the flies—and at you. It's had lots of shoes put on its feet, but it knows you're new at the business and figures that if it doesn't see an opportunity to kick your ass halfway across the barn, it'll sure as hell bite a big hunk out of the seat of those brand new Levis.

Besides, Wass yelled a lot. The man was able to see mistakes from a hundred yards away that I was desperately trying to hide.

"You wasp any mowe off dat hoof, dat hoss gonna bleed to death."

Or, "Goddamnit Won, time you get awound to nailin dem shoes on, dat hoss's hooves gonna be all gwoan out again and he'll need to be we-shod!" (The normal horse's hooves grow at a rate of approximately one-eighth of an inch per month.)

About the same time that I'd decided that if God had intended for horses to wear shoes He'd have taught them to lie on their backs and hold their feet up quietly, things began to get better. Instead of two and a half hours, I got to where I could shoe a horse in just over an hour. My hands were beginning to heal a little, and I hadn't driven a nail into my thigh in nearly a week. I remember thinking how I was going to delight and amaze city slickers with my newly acquired skill.

While it's true that in horseshoer's school the scholar who applies himself diligently can achieve the technical skill it takes to nail a shoe on a horse's foot, and can even memorize the names of the equine bones and ligaments below the knee, there are several equally important skills that come with having suc-

51

cessfully completed the requirements for the Basic Farrier Certificate from one of the nation's leading institutions of higher learning. Whereas the fundamental theory and the practical application of the farrier's art are taught formally, according to a strict curriculum, the other skills to which I refer come gradually—you might even say they sneak up on you. Two examples are the Trampled-Toe Two-Step, and the Skoal Brother Dribble.

The Trampled-Toe Two-Step is a distinct way of walking that reveals to those initiated few that one is, indeed, a working farrier. While painful to describe, the TTTS proceeds from the hypothesis that you hurt real bad (usually true)—that your back is irreparably bent, your toes maimed beyond recognition by ungrateful horses stomping their shiny new shoes down smartly on your Tony Lama's, and your ass is dragging. Once you see an advanced case of this affliction, you'll never forget it. In fact, you may wake up screaming some nights just dreaming about how it must feel.

And then there's the phenomenon of the Skoal Brother Dribble. Horseshoers dip snuff. It's as simple as that. I don't know why, they just do. And they were doing so long before former Dallas Cowboy football hero Walt Garrison decided to put a "peench" between his "cheek and gum" prior to wrestling steers on television commercials. Shit, real horseshoers know that a "dip" goes down inside your bottom lip—and they also know that a dip is about a half pound of the nasty stuff, and not any "peench."

You may have noticed that horseshoers also hold nails in their mouths while they tack on the shoes. And when they've got ahold of a particularly fidgety horse—and most horses are fidgety when they're getting their feet hammered on—the shoer gets mad and his salivary glands (stimulated by his anger and that big wad of slobbery tobacco) go into overdrive. Naturally the nails in his mouth make it difficult, if not impossible, to spit, and . . . well, you get the picture. Skoal Brother Dribble.

On Graduation Day NMSU Farrier Science Course Class #46 held the traditional Farrier's Free-For-All down on the

Ron back when he was a practicing farrier

riverbank. There were wash tubs filled with iced beer, water-melons, hot dogs, Fritos, and Pecan Sandies.

And rain. There came a record-breaking toad strangler, so twenty people jammed together in two pickup campers and listened to 8-track tapes of Merle Haggard and the Strangers while sipping on cold cans of Bud and dipping snuff. (Those green-horns who hadn't yet mastered the delicate art of dippin' and drinkin' at the same time smoked Bull Durham roll-your-owns.)

Later on, as I drove the three hundred and some miles home, scarred and fifteen pounds lighter than when I'd left, I thought about the wonderful new life-style my $30,000-a-year income would afford me.

On Monday morning I placed classified ads in the local news-paper, had 2,000 business cards printed up with an eye-catching picture of a horseshoe, and visited all the larger horse-breeding farms in the county. Oh, but I was eager.

I spent about six months as a working farrier. Six months during which I was daily kicked, stepped, stomped, shit, and chewed on. I made some money. Not as much as I'd hoped . . . I figure another eighteen or twenty years of full-time work might have pushed me over that $30,000 mark if my back held up.

I did find out just why it was I used to have to wait for a month or more to get a horseshoer. I had naturally thought they were all booked up—like a dentist. The truth is, the poor bastards just couldn't bear the thought of facing another one of those backyard pets. Even the most ill-mannered, spoiled, and obnoxious only child can't begin to compare with the pampered hobby-horse. Worse yet is the once-a-year deer hunter's pack horse—used for maybe three days in the fall and then turned out to roam free until the next year when, madder than a hornet, he's hazed up toward the first human being he's seen in twelve months—a mere mortal armed only with a hammer, a mouthful of nails and tobacco, and $175 worth of schooling. Then, two hours later, the owner of this sorry outlaw pisses and moans about the cost of the job while he whines that in the good old days a durned farrier would shoe upwards of fifty wild mules a day for two bits apiece. And with that he hands what too often turns out to be a postdated check written on an overdrawn account to the bruised and bleeding farrier.

Now, I ask you, Is it any wonder that the good men who set out to shoe America's horses wind up drinking and cussing and eventually turn *mean*?

My friend A. T. once told me that he figured the perfect horseshoer was built like a cigarette machine and retired at an early age.

I'm not and I did.

EIGHT

Why I Gave up Dipping Snuff

A CULTURED LADY OF MY ACQUAINTANCE
asked me recently if I would explain to her all about chewing
and dipping tobacco. She had rightly deduced from reading the
foregoing account of how I chanced to become a famous horseshoer that I now, or at least did at one time, dip snuff. She
claimed that it is a great mystery to "all women and most men"
just why it is people do that.

I should begin by pointing out that this lady clearly does not
travel in livestock and agricultural circles. If she did, she would
surely have noticed that it is not at all an uncommon sight at
rural American county fairs and calf ropings to see a good
many otherwise attractive young women—uniformly attired in
breathtakingly tight Wranglers decorated with fancy leather
belts sporting hand-tooled advertisements of the wearer's first
name on the back and fastened with silver trophy buckles the
size of hubcaps—dipping Skoal or Copenhagen, the most popular brands of snuff. And of course everyone knows that it
would be remarkable to see even *one* of the young men at such
cowboy attractions who did *not* have a big lipful of tobacco.

I'll confess that I don't know why otherwise intelligent folks
dip snuff any more than I understand why seemingly bright
folks smoke cigarettes. (My guess is that increasingly fewer
people do either.) I was a smoker, more or less continually, for

a good twenty-five years. What's more—and at the same time, I might add—I was a confirmed dipper of snuff for probably five of those years. I suppose I took up smoking because it was the thing to do back when I was a greasy-haired teenager. I loved smoking. I took up dipping, like I said, because I couldn't smoke and shoe horses at the same time. Putting tobacco in your mouth and holding it there for long periods of time is just as habit-forming—indeed, addictive—as is smoking cigarettes. The physiological (psychological?) attraction of inhaling smoke and of absorbing nicotine through the mucous membranes of one's mouth is surprisingly similar—the light-headed rush of one's first cigarette compares strikingly with that first dip of snuff. I loved dipping snuff.

Always the gentleman, however—and cognizant of the fact that some of your more squeamish types take umbrage at the sight of the tell-tale lumpy lip of the advanced dipper—when I started seeing Elaine I made it a point not to dip (and so spit) in her presence. After we were married it became clear that, as working ranchers, we were destined continually to be together and so if I wanted to maintain my conjugal right to the occasional kiss on the mouth, I was going to have to take to strolling out behind the barn to enjoy my Skoal . . . that, or give up my addiction altogether.

When one is in the bloom of love it is easier to kick old habits than at any other time, I believe. Which is to say, I gave up dipping snuff. I did not—immediately, anyway—give up smoking. Elaine smokes . . . like a stack. (She does not dip— never has, as far as I know.) As I get older and so more attuned to health issues, and the durned Surgeon General just keeps making me nervouser and nervouser with all his warnings and discoveries about how dangerous everything is, Elaine's smoking worries me more and more. Anyway, after we'd been married about a year, I figured it was time to quit. I solemnly announced to Elaine that I was going to avoid any further risk of cancer by once and for all ridding my body of nasty nicotine deposits and all the sticky accumulations of tar. I magnanimously added that I wouldn't object or nag if she continued to

"The Happy Rancher" ("Just a peench between cheek and gum")

smoke; however, I very much wanted her to remain healthy and so it seemed like a real good time for her to quit, as well. Naturally I assumed she would join me in my crusade for clean lungs.

I guess the bloom of love thing I mentioned is an individual attribute. Anyway, Elaine surprised me by taking me at my pious word that I wouldn't nag. . . . She kept on smoking.

I've got to confess that I backslid a little myself, though. What with Elaine puffing away, my effort to quit smoking was more difficult than I'd imagined. I told my wife that since I was just trying to avoid lung cancer anyway, I figured it wouldn't hurt to ease my withdrawal pain with an occasional dip of "Smokeless Tobacco." I guess she felt a little guilty about her unwillingness to join with me in tossing away the cigarettes, because she didn't object to that.

Then a couple of months later I remember we were sitting on the couch minding our own business, holding hands and watching *60 Minutes* on television. You may have seen the segment . . . it was about how dipping snuff causes cancer. Mike Wallace or Andy Rooney or somebody showed ghastly pictures of young people who, because they dipped snuff, had their faces half eaten away.

Elaine still smokes.* I don't. I don't smoke, or dip, or do anything that's fun anymore. I just take lots of vitamins and watch my cholesterol intake.

You'll be pleased to learn that since this writing Miss Elaine has stopped smoking.

NINE

Where the Deer
and the Antelope Roam

SOME TIME BACK I READ THAT A FAMOUS professional anthropologist had figured out that the Plains Indians used to hunt antelope. That they used to hunt them on *foot*. Now I don't know about you, but I was skeptical when I read that, seeing as how every antelope I ever came across could easily outrun a Toyota. But according to this guy, some alert Indian had noticed that antelope are extremely curious animals and discovered that if he lay on his back in the grass and kicked his legs up in the air, any antelope in the general vicinity wouldn't be able to stand the suspense and would have to come up close to see what in the world this guy was doing—thus making it relatively easy for other members of the tribe to shoot their arrows into "Mr. Curious."

I bring this up because when I first met Elaine I remember being astonished by the large number of pronghorn antelope that hung out on her ranch. Of course it wasn't unusual to see antelope in that part of East Central New Mexico—in fact, you could say it would be remarkable *not* to see them when driving through the sheep country between, say, Vaughn and Roswell. But Lake Ranch was cut in half by I-40, like I said. And although the six thousand acres that made up our front yard may seem like a sizeable spread to some folks, it's not really what you'd call a major wildlife preserve—at least not when you add a house and a bunch of outbuildings, a couple of smelly pickup trucks, and two barking dogs. Then, like I say, bisect it with a four-lane highway that moves sun-burned tourists in hippie vans and Winnebagos between Chicago and L.A. I mean, there's got to be a lot of less populated places around that I would have thought more appealing to antelope.

I suppose a lot of it goes back to the fact that Elaine's grandfather—and she after him—wouldn't allow hunting on the ranch. As I understand it, the man would go out of his way not to disturb the wildlife that shared title to his land—rattlesnakes and coyotes not withstanding. He'd give wide berth to a herd of antelope, and particularly to any doe he'd see off by herself where she might be giving birth to, or at least protecting by hiding, her kids. Elaine tells how once when she was very small, she remembers her grandfather came across a pair of orphaned antelope kids, brought them up to the milking barn, and bottle-fed them until they were big enough to join up with some of their own kind. Sadly, when her grandfather released the twins, one got confused and ran back toward the pens and into a fence, breaking its neck. She says, however, that even as a full-grown buck, the other would come up to her grandfather out in the pasture when he was feeding the cattle. I wish I'd seen that.

Anyway, whenever I used to drive in the front gate of the ranch and bounce the couple of miles down the rutted dirt road toward the house, I could always count on seeing a good number of antelope—*whether* I'd see them was never the question, but rather how *many* I would see. As I recall, the most I ever counted at one time was a herd of more than seventy animals.

I remember being especially taken with the way the antelope would act at night, when I'd be taking Elaine home after one of our rare trips to Santa Fe when we were courting, or when I'd be heading back out to Puerto de Luna after watching Johnny Carson's monologue on the big color television set she had.

It seemed as though the antelope were irresistibly drawn to my moving truck. What's more, they obviously took great delight in racing along the road beside me as I drove. And what

Orphaned Antelope, Summer, 1957

was most curious to me was that the object of the race—at least as far as the antelope were concerned—looked to be for them to handily outrun the truck and then to cross in front of me and laughingly (or so I imagined) make their escape into the darkness. You understand, this feat was not especially difficult, given the condition of my truck and that of the driveway. And even though I'm told pronghorn antelope have been observed to reach speeds of up to sixty miles an hour for short intervals, I'll confess no one claims ever to have observed my pickup going anywhere near that fast. It should come as no great surprise then, that in all the times I was party or witness to one of these "races," the antelope never failed to win.

Another thing that struck me was this: Given the seemingly irresistible urge of the antelope to cross in front of a moving vehicle, coupled with the fact that ordinary livestock fence presents absolutely no barrier to them, I would have thought it not remarkable to occasionally see the remains of antelope along the Interstate where they have to contend with far more formidable opponents than me and a Toyota pickup that needs a valve job bouncing along a deeply rutted caliche driveway. I for one, however, have never seen where an antelope has been hit along a highway.

On the other hand, there are coyotes. I mean, it's certainly no secret that coyotes are among the wiliest creatures to be found anywhere outside the halls of Congress—and I don't know about you, but I've sure often enough seen the grisly evidence of where *those* critters have been mashed flat by big shiny cabover Peterbilt eighteen-wheelers.

I just don't understand how antelope escape the same fate. Elaine maintains that it's because antelope are *nice* animals—that coyotes, on the other hand, are wicked and evil creatures and therefore *deserve* to be stepped on, kicked, choked, beat up, run over, shot, stabbed, poisoned, and then hung up on fence posts as a serious warning to other coyotes not to get their ass caught comin' around *this* property! (While I've known her to sit up night after freezing night with a snot-nosed dogied calf, and to weep unashamedly at the sight of a big-eyed skinny horse bound for the dogfood factory as it passed through a public sale ring, Elaine is not what you'd call a bleeding heart animal rights activist when it comes to coyotes.)

We have coyotes where we live now. Which shouldn't be all that surprising—I understand they have coyotes in downtown Beverly Hills, for chrissake! I don't know about you, but I'm convinced that coyotes and ticks are all that's gonna be left on earth after the Big Bang finally comes. Them and maybe some mesquite trees.

Talking about antelope just naturally makes me think of the time when I was out walking alone on the ranch and came across a medium-sized antelope grazing off all by himself. It happened to be late summer—which is the antelope rutting season—and I figured this guy had been chased off from a band of females in heat by a larger, more popular buck—possibly even the captain of the football team. Naturally, I felt an immediate kinship with him. Anyway, he was maybe a couple of hundred yards away, and stood very still and looked at me. It occurred to me that I might ought to try out the old leg-waving method of luring him up for a closer look. I slowly sat down and, being careful to avoid the cactus and any rattlesnake that might be lurking in the area, lay back and began to kick my legs in the air—much in the manner of the old "bicycle" exercise that Coach Ennis Hoskins used to require back at Ponca Military Academy in Oklahoma when I was a high school athlete there.

I kept this up for about five minutes, thinking all the while how proud Coach Hoskins would be that I wasn't even breathing hard. Then I heard what sounded to me like voices. Actually, it *was* voices—it was Denzil Calhoun from the next place over along with his brother-in-law, Emil Finney. They happened to be passing through our pasture on horseback on their way to check on some of our common boundary fence.

"Howdy," said Emil.

Denzil grinned. "Afternoon, neighbor." He looked down to where I'd been laying in the weeds. "Gettin' kindly a dry, ain't it?"

(You'll note that the sorry bastards did not have the courtesy to inquire as to whether I'd been thrown from my horse and was hurt or suffering from sunstroke or something. Rather they chose to let me squirm and stutter in red-faced embarrassment.)

I promptly assumed what I hoped was a pained expression and, placing my hands on my hips, began bending from side to side in the faint hope that they would deduce that my well-known gimpy back had gone out on me once more, and I had thoughtfully come clear out in the pasture to suffer so as not to cause undue alarm to my new bride.

"Yeah," I mumbled. "We could sure enough stand a little moisture headin' into winter."

The two men looked me up and down once more, grinned at one another and clucked to their horses.

"Say 'Hey' to Miss Elaine," snickered Denzil Calhoun.

"Y'all come see us," chortled Emil Finney.

Sure, thought I. *Fat chance I'm gonna come callin' on you bastards.*

Still, I managed a half-hearted wave as the two men rode away. Then I started walking back toward the house. I never thought to look and see where that buck had gone.

TEN

Looking for Trouble

I SUPPOSE I SHOULD TELL YOU THAT, TO this day, Elaine thinks I'm just being silly about all this, and has said as much in public. I suppose she may be right. She maintains that a lot of folks have had at least one calf that's been a headache from the very start.

Ours was named "Trouble." My wife, in what I can only describe as a moment of spooky clairvoyance, named him that the day he was born. I've read of studies that suggest humans have a tendency to assume those characteristics that have become, over the years, associated with their given names . . . partly, I guess, because others tend to respond to a certain name according to the stereotypical image that that particular name conjures up. (You can't tell me, for example, that you picture the same person when I say "Bubba" or "Wanda June" as you do when I say "Roger" or "Marsha.") So maybe Elaine's responsible for everything I'm about to tell you . . . I don't know.

The trouble with Trouble started even before he was born. But I'm getting ahead of myself. . . .

You already know how I happened to come to the cattle business rather late in life, and that I had to learn a lot of things that those raised up around cows take for granted. Like how to pull a calf, for instance.

When Elaine and I got married, she had thirteen heifers due

67

to deliver their first calves any day. I figured natural calfbirth would proceed routinely. After all, it was summertime, and the animals looked fat and healthy. What problems could possibly arise?

So when Elaine casually mentioned one morning over coffee that I'd better be sure I had the "calf puller" in the truck whenever I checked the heifers, I'll admit I was taken aback.

Oh sure, I've helped horses foal out often enough. If a mare appears to be having difficulty in giving birth, I know how to take careful hold of the foal's front legs and gently pull in unison with the mare's contractions in order to help her along. And it's true that sometimes one has to put an arm up inside the mare in order to help reposition the foal so that it might be delivered properly. But all of this is accomplished in the relative cleanliness and comfort of a well-bedded foaling barn, with veterinary supplies and an emergency telephone close at hand. Listen . . . my wife was talking about me using a "calf puller"—which I took to be some sort of *machine*—and using it out in a lonely and remote *pasture*!

She explained that first-calving heifers have a long-standing tradition of difficult births. That one of the livestock books she had said that about one in three young heifers experiences enough of a problem that she requires assistance in becoming a mother cow.

Our calf puller was really just a bumper jack—like the thing used to change a tire—with a brace at one end that fits up against the mother-to-be's rear, and a chain that fastens around the calf-to-be's front leg or legs—depending on what you can see or get a grip on. Then, whoever's operating the device pumps on the handle (as though jacking up a car) and so "pulls" the calf. I've since heard of cattlemen who, coming upon a cow needing help delivering her calf and not being fortunate enough to have one of these modern conveniences in the truck, will simply tie a rope or tow-chain to the calf's feet, attach the other end to the bumper, and drive off.

At the time, I assumed that the use of a calf puller was limited to heroic, life-saving, last-ditch efforts and occurred maybe

once in a lifetime; surely Elaine had just inherited another antique curiosity that she was using to kid me with. (Like the out-
house that stood out by the chicken coop and caused me to
keep my first couple of visits relatively brief back when we
were first courting—until I discovered the ranch house had indoor facilities just like big city places.)

But my bride assured me that I might truly need the calf
puller, so I put it all together as best I could figure, and squirted
oil on all the moving parts and tossed it in the back of the
pickup along with the traditional part roll of barbed wire, the
set of post-hole diggers, and the half-sack of cattle feed. (The
barbed wire and post-hole diggers make it look like you'd be
ready to mend some fence if you could just find a place to start,
and the feed—commonly called cake—is in case you need to
lure some livestock somewhere they might otherwise not wish
to go.) Looking back, I realize now that I was secretly pleased
when I saw folks admiring the calf puller whenever we went to
the feedstore or the bank. I liked to imagine they figured I'd
used the thing and so must have been one hell of a cowboy.

The first heifer calved without a hitch. At least I don't think
she had any problem. When I first saw her calf it was, experience tells me now, four or five days old, so well had she hidden
her new baby from my greenhorn eyes. One down and twelve
to go. No sweat.

A couple of days later I had spent the better part of the
morning filling the stock trailer with more junk—trying all the
while to avoid the rattlesnakes and black widows that lurked in
the fifty-year-old piles of tires and wire. I had the trailer loaded
beyond what is legal for highway travel, I'm sure, and had
bribed Elaine with the promise of a Dairy Queen to go with me
to the Santa Rosa dump.

We were about halfway out to the mailbox when Elaine spotted one of the heifers way off by herself. We watched her
through the binoculars we keep on the dashboard for just such
occasions.

My heart sank when Elaine told me it was Gypsy. I was not

then—nor am I now—overly fond of Gypsy. She was a goosey, high-headed Brangus-Charolais cross that would have been downright dangerous had she not been so stupid.

We watched Gypsy lie down for a little while, and then get up and walk around for a couple of minutes and then lie down again. We knew enough not to disturb her if we could help it, but after nearly an hour, I figured we might do well to try and get a closer look. I unhitched the trailer in the middle of the road and tried to drive slowly and quietly toward where she was.

Gypsy saw us coming right off; she jumped up and ran two hundred yards to a little clump of cactus and tried to hide behind it. While she was running away from us, we could plainly see the front legs of her calf protruding from under her tail. (I know that's what it was, because Elaine told me.)

I stopped the truck; Elaine waited while I tried to tiptoe real nonchalant-like toward Gypsy. Pretending that I was just out for an afternoon stroll, admiring nature, and that I had no interest whatsoever in cattle. She didn't buy it for a minute. Spotting the rest of the herd about a quarter of a mile away, she galloped off to join them. By then it had been almost two hours since we'd first discovered her; we had no idea how long before that she might have been trying to calve.

Right about then Gypsy lay down and began to strain again. I gathered up the calf puller and, hunkering down on all fours like I'd learned to do in Marine Corps boot camp, tried crawling toward her like she was a godless communist in a machine gun nest. She jumped up and ran as soon as I was close enough to see that the water bag had torn and the calf's leg was nearly dry. I told Elaine I didn't think that was a good sign. Drastic measures were in order.

I put a "peench" of Skoal between my cheek and gum like Walt Garrison says to do on television, took the lariat from behind the seat, and crawled up into the bed of the pickup. I let out a sizeable loop and instructed Elaine to maneuver close to Gypsy. I wish to this day my wife had thought to bring her camera along that morning, or at least to have notified the crew

from "Wide World of Sports" to be on hand: I got the cow
with my first try—and I don't mean my first try that day. I
mean my first try *ever*—and expertly dallied to the rusty trailer
hitch ball on the bumper.

So proud of my new-found skill was I at that moment, I figured I might just have to sign up for the National Finals Rodeo
in the Championship Heifer Roping event. I quit grinning when
Gypsy went bananas.

When she'd struggled enough that she'd finally pulled the
noose so tight that she choked down and fell to her side, I
jumped down out of the truck and looped the calf puller chain
around the protruding calf's foot and started pumping the jack
handle. I hollered at Elaine to back up a couple of feet so as to
give the strangling, bug-eyed cow a little slack and maybe a
breath of oxygen. As I pumped the handle on the puller, Gypsy
regained about a third of what little wits she had and started
struggling to her feet. By then I had the calf's head out and I
guess the point was beginning to come across to Gypsy. She
stood fairly still and even began to push a little while I jacked
the handle. Once the shoulders were delivered, the cow went
down again. With a little more effort from Gypsy and a final
jerk on the calf puller, the baby came with a loud *whoosh.*

I picked the slippery calf up by its hind legs and shook it as
hard as I could—I either read somewhere that one was supposed to do that, or else it came to me in a vision at that very
moment. Elaine, meanwhile, hollered at me that she was sure
Gypsy was dead or dying. I dropped the calf and removed the
noose from around Gypsy's neck. I barely escaped being tram-
pled to death when she leapt up and ran off to where her sister
cows were watching a distance away.

We went back to work on the calf—shaking it around some
more—and shortly it seemed to be breathing okay. The new
mother was off grazing with the rest of the herd and trying to
act like she didn't have anything to do with all the commotion.
I began to get the sinking feeling that what we had on our
hands was a dogie—a calf rejected by its natural mother.

Fortunately, there was that half-sack of cake in the pickup bed

Gypsy and her hour-old calf, Trouble

that Domino hadn't eaten yet—cake being one of his favorite things next to horny toads—and we managed to lure the entire bunch over to where the still wet calf was lying by shaking the sack and hollering "Whooo-eee" like cowpersons do when they're luring cattle around. Some of the smarter heifers started sniffing at the baby, but Gypsy was sure that I had some new and unspeakable torture in mind and so kept her distance. We backed off to watch.

After about twenty minutes, Gypsy eased over for a wary inspection of what it was the others found so interesting. Apparently Mother Nature triggered some kind of maternal instinct because the new momma began to lick her calf and, after just a couple of minutes of licking, to chase the other heifers away.

I don't want you to get the wrong impression here. Gypsy never was what you'd call a good mother. In fact, while I have no proof, I honestly believe that on several occasions she tried to pawn her baby off on some other, unsuspecting cow. The others, however, seemed to want baby Trouble even less than his own momma did.

A couple of months later we had a half-dozen bull calves in the bunch with Trouble, two of which we'd had to "pull": so much for my antique curiosity theory. We picked a nice day to brand and cut the calves . . . I considered myself an old salt by then, so we didn't call up the old timer from Albuquerque or any of those other folks.

The first couple of days after castration are the most crucial for the new little steers. You have to watch to be sure there's no bad swelling and that your victims don't get stiff-legged or otherwise exhibit untoward signs of complications. After about the third day you don't have to worry too much.

On the fourth day, I couldn't find Trouble.

I swear I drove over every inch of the pasture. I found Gypsy, placidly grazing with the others, not in the least concerned that her baby was missing. After two hours of searching, I got off a ways from Gypsy and tried to make noises like a calf in distress. A good mother cow will usually at least look in the direction of where her baby is when she hears those sounds. Not being a good mother, Gypsy just kept on grazing.

I went back up to the house and got Elaine; we searched for another hour. I'd about decided that we'd been hit by rustlers when my eagle-eyed wife spotted Trouble all hunkered down in the middle of a cedar bush. We drove up beside him.

He was so swollen, it appeared as though he'd grown a small watermelon between his legs. And he was so stiff-legged he could barely move. We were at least a mile and a half from the herd and Trouble's aloof mother.

I climbed out and started slowly hazing the calf in the general direction of the herd while Elaine followed in the truck. It took over an hour to make the journey. But except to spook from me and the truck, Gypsy didn't seem to notice our arrival.

We went back to the house to have some coffee and to read up on postcastration complications in the Livestock Handbook. When we went back out, Trouble—exhausted and trying his

best to die—was lying in a heap of cactus. I sat on his head so
Elaine could give him a big dose of antibiotics. Then I took my
pocket knife and opened up the original incision site, hoping to
drain off some of the crud and corruption that was threatening
to kill the calf.

We performed this operation every morning for five days.
Each morning, as we prepared to go out to search for Trouble,
I tried to console my tender-hearted wife by telling her that she
shouldn't feel depressed and guilty should we find him dead:
we'd done everything possible to save him, and there was probably more grass in calf heaven than in Guadalupe County, anyway.

We didn't find him dead. On about the seventh or eighth day,
Trouble looked to be a little better. But for the next week or
so, he refused to have anything to do with his own species.
Since his mother didn't seem to care much about looking after
him, I spent a good part of each day locating him and then hazing him toward the rest of the herd.

Trouble had lost quite a bit of weight and looked so poor I
was afraid he might wander up near the Interstate where a passing motorist would see him and report me for calf abuse to the
Humane Society. I figured if I could keep him out of sight and
alive for just a little while longer, maybe I could get him to the
sale and he wouldn't be a total loss. (I don't know about yours,
but our livestock insurance paid off only if the animal was
struck by lightning or hit by a car; I told Elaine that if we
found Trouble dead she didn't have to watch but I was going to
run over his body a couple of times and tearfully tell the agent
in Santa Rosa that he just came out of nowhere and I couldn't
stop in time.)

But Trouble survived. He still had a big knot between his
back legs, but he began to pick up weight and started mixing
with the other calves. Naturally, I got lazy and didn't take him
to the sale.

When they were about six months old, we weaned our thirteen calves. Elained checked in the *Farmers Almanac* to see that
the "signs" were right before we took the calves away from

Trouble

their mommas. I don't really believe that the "signs" have anything to do with it, you understand, but Elaine suggested I not
be too proud to accept help—from whatever source.

The weaning went very well. There was the usual amount of
bawling from both the babies and their mothers—except for
Gypsy, who seemed not to notice that anything different was
happening.

But on the third day—actually it was the third night, and it
was snowing—fortunes reversed themselves.

When I went out to check on the weanlings before bed, I
found that Trouble sort of stood out from the rest of the
weaners in that he was blown up like a hot-air balloon. He was
grotesquely bloated, unable even to walk. (If you'd like an ex-
planation of why cows bloat, there are any number of books to
read and animal experts to ask. Me, I just know it's something
that happens and leave it at that.)

75

Elaine bundled up and we went out to see if maybe we couldn't get him to move around a little. No *way*, José Ganadero.

Elaine had never had a case of bloat on the place; I had about as much notion of what to do as if I'd been assigned to perform delicate brain surgery. I called up A. T., who'd been in the cattle business before he got intelligent and switched over to horses.

He told me unless I wanted a dead cow-critter on my hands, I was going to have to stick a knife in the calf's rumen—that's one of its stomachs—to deflate him. (To tell the truth, sticking a knife in its side sounded to me like a pretty good way of ending up with a dead critter. But then I've already admitted to being new at this.) A. T. suggested I might want to try poking a garden hose down the calf's throat before I stabbed him. I asked him if that was a joke—he said no, but that if the garden hose didn't relieve the gas I should go ahead and stab him, and if *that* didn't work I'd at least be on the way to butchering him and dressing him out for the freezer.

Elaine got the pickup while I cut a six-foot length of hose, and we went up to where the weaners were penned. It took awhile, but we got the bloated Trouble into the squeeze chute. Even with the chute completely open, it was still a tight fit. We parked the truck to where I could see by the headlights and I poked the hose down the calf's throat.

It worked.

Boy, did it work! With all the gas that came shooting out of that hose, I'm surprised Trouble didn't fly off backwards like one of those party balloons you'd blow up and then release so it'd crazily fly all around the room when you were a kid. When we pulled the hose out of his mouth, Trouble was normal-sized again. In fact, he turned completely around in the chute he'd been squeezed into and pranced happily back into the pen with his buddies.

I'm told that if a cow bloats once, it's a good bet it'll do so again. No question about it, Elaine may have gotten overly attached to Trouble—what with all the doctoring and worrying over him—but he was going to the sale! The worrisome little shit had tried to die on me since the day he was born, and was beginning to make me paranoid. I figured that with his (and my) luck, he'd leap out of the trailer in a desperate suicide attempt out on the Interstate between Lake Ranch and Clovis, wiping out a school bus filled with nuns and little orphan children on their way to town for ice cream.

Either that or he'd trip coming out of the trailer at the sale yard and break his neck. Then the yard foreman would charge me an arm and a leg just to drag Trouble's carcass out of the line of catcalling cowboys waiting to unload their well-behaved steers.

We finally got Trouble loaded up and taken down to Clovis on the day before the regular sale. Our normal practice was to take the stock down early on Wednesday morning and make a day of it: lunch at the Cattlemen's Cafe, watch cows go through the sale ring all afternoon, and maybe get a Big Mac and fries for the trip home that evening. (Now, that may not sound like a big time to you, but then you probably get decent television reception and can get pizza delivered right to your door.)

This time, however, we went down on Tuesday and just abandoned Trouble to be sold the following day. I've often wondered what happened to the poor, innocent son-of-a-bitch who bought him.

The next morning, over coffee, Elaine told me about a dream she'd had: that Trouble had busted out of the pens and led all the cattle and a good many sheep in a mass escape from the Clovis Stockyards.

It was awful, she said. Bawling and bleating, they were running wild through the streets of town—breaking store windows and setting fires . . . drinking beer . . . raping and pillaging. Not only that, the authorities had solid evidence proving *our* calf was the leader of this gang of miscreants—that they'd hoof-cuffed him and taken him to the slammer—and we were being held personally responsible for the whole, ugly incident.

It was several days before I could persuade my wife, and my-self, that it was really just a bad dream . . . that such a thing couldn't happen. At least not in America.

ELEVEN

On Doctoring Livestock

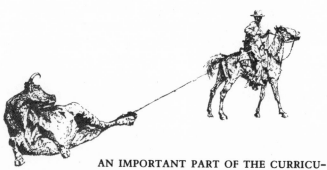

AN IMPORTANT PART OF THE CURRICU-
lum at any major veterinary college in this country is surely
that course aimed at teaching aspiring young DVMs how best
to dupe their client into believing that all his valuable livestock
will undoubtedly die a slow and painful death due to screw-
worm infestation or hoof-and-mouth disease or something
equally ghastly unless he agrees to fork over an amount equal to
the price of a new Ford pickup truck three or four times a year
to have the vet come out to the ranch and personally lay his
healing hands upon every animal on the place. *Preventive medicine,* the veterinary colleges call it.

But when you find yourself trying to grow cows and raise
horses on a place seventy-five or a hundred miles from the nearest clinic, you soon learn that should you need the on-site help
of a veterinarian at any time other than those regularly scheduled afternoons when he's there giving shots and drinking coffee anyway, you're better off trying to make do on your own.
Like when the enthusiastic young freedom fighters from the Air
Force Base over at Clovis are out practicing napalming Communists by buzzing what they consider sparsely populated areas
and playfully run your best colt through a barbed wire fence
and it needs to be sewn back together and the vet's not scheduled to visit your part of the state for six months. In that case,

the most you can expect is some advice over the telephone—
and that only if your vet is one of those rare liberals who considers you an intelligent enough individual to follow simple instructions. More than likely, however, you'll find yourself
directed to somehow get the frightened and bleeding animal
loaded into your trailer and haul it on over to Santa Fe. (Speak-
ing of making do, I don't want to get him in trouble with the
AMA or whoever it is that keeps an alert eye out for know-it-
all malcontents who risk imprisonment by practicing veterinary
medicine without a license, but I've observed my friend A. T.
sew up some of the nastiest wire cuts and gaping wounds you'd
ever hope to see on a young horse. I still marvel at his patience
and skill in doing so.)

All of which is meant to help explain why Elaine and I, like
most ranchers, were so often giving shots to or worming or
otherwise doctoring everything on our place with four legs and
some with just two.

It's not surprising that vets want us to think there's some secret formula—some magic method of giving a cow a vaccina-
tion—that is revealed to them at a secret ceremony during the
second semester of their senior year at college. I mean, veterinarians got a fraternal obligation to triple the price they
charge for Blackleg Vaccine and otherwise practice free enterprise so they can buy themselves fancy new vehicles every six
months and big houses just like physicians and lawyers.

But I'm here to tell you that there ain't nothing magic about
giving shots. I know, because I've done it about a million times.
So, naturally when Elaine's favorite cat somehow got a small
wound that looked like maybe it was beginning to abscess and
could maybe use some antibiotics, I figured I had all the on-the-
job medical training that was necessary. I should point out that
part of my figuring was based on the fact that when I married
Elaine she already owned an ancient part-Siamese who, she
liked to brag, was a two-hundred-dollar cat ever since an owl
or a hawk or something else big and mean had caught her nap-
ping and tried to have the sorry old thing for lunch and then

some prissy cat doctor over in Clovis had charged two hundred dollars just to lay his healing hands on her.

Anyway, this other cat—Fearless is its name, and I can only say that names just kind of happen to our animals—was one that Elaine got me to agree to legally adopt only after she'd tearfully explained how some woman in town had discovered this whole litter of precious little orphaned kittens in an alley— nearly starved and too young even to have opened their eyes. Supposedly, this good Samaritan had snatched the little tykes from the very jaws of death and then personally bottle-fed them every hour for six weeks or something equally heroic. This woman also claimed to know a whole lot about kittens—which is to say, she professed to be able to distinguish the males from the females. I told Elaine that I'd agree to getting another cat only if she'd promise to choose a short-haired male.

You've probably already guessed that she came home with a long-haired female. Elaine still maintains that both she and the expert thought this particular kitten was a male. In fact, my wife held fast to her claim that Fearless was a boy until just recently—she finally gave in when the fresh young vet down the road charged us fifty-five dollars to spay him. (You'll note that I still call her "him.")

When Elaine noticed one day that Fearless had a wound about the size of a dime on his shoulder, she figured maybe it ought to be attended to. She said that the vet who'd treated the old two-hundred-dollar cat had given her a shot of penicillin and cleaned the wound good (that was just before he retired to the Bahamas, you understand).

Of course we had plenty of animal drugs and medicines on hand, and I knew from experience exactly what the prescribed dosage of penicillin was for a two-thousand-pound bull and a twelve-hundred-pound mare. All I had to do was get out my calculator to figure out how much I should give a four-pound cat. Then I cleared off a place on the kitchen table and gathered up some peroxide, A&D ointment, Q-tips, and cotton balls while Elaine went out and caught Fearless.

We wrapped our feline patient in a clean towel so that when he got scared he wouldn't be as likely to scratch and claw at either of us. I figured that administering the antibiotic was the most necessary part of this whole procedure, so I suggested to Elaine that I ought to give the shot first just in case Fearless got hysterical and we couldn't hold him down. I'll admit that Elaine exhibited some skepticism when she noticed that I intended to use the same size needle on Fearless that I used on the cows. I patiently explained that this was the only size we had on hand and that I didn't intend to plunge the whole thing into her precious little cat, thank you very much. (If it sounds like I was getting a little testy, it's because I was secretly concerned over the size of the needle myself.) I gently felt around on the cat's rear end, looking for the proper deep muscle in which to give the shot.

Let's stop right here for a minute. If you have a cat handy, I'd like to you to get up right now and go see if you can find a place anywhere on its body that even remotely resembles that fleshy part of your anatomy where the nurse gave you your last shot of penicillin. Ain't no such place, is there?

I did the best I could . . . Really, I did.

Fearless didn't act like he was too upset. He didn't holler or try to get away. In fact, he was being so still that Elaine and I made a big fuss over how brave he was being. And because he was being so good, I went on ahead and cleaned and doctored the wound.

"What a good kitty!"

I was feeling particularly cocky over having probably just saved us a giant vet bill while, at the same time, having provided further evidence to Elaine of how very fortunate she was to have found herself such an all-around talented husband to look after her and all the livestock. I told her she could let Fearless up now.

"Come on, Sweetie," she was saying in the voice she uses to talk to her animals. "It's all better now."

Fearless

I have to report that the cat just lay there—looking fairly despondent and staring at Elaine.

She picked him up off the table.

It was kind of like picking up a limp dish-rag—Fearless looked to be paralyzed from right about the ears down.

He was breathing. And it was fairly obvious that he could still see. But he couldn't stand . . . or walk. Like I said, he was just *limp*.

Naturally, the first thought I had was that it was a horrible reaction to the penicillin. (Actually, it was the *second* thought I had. The first thing I remember thinking was that I'd screwed up again and murdered my wife's favorite pet, and how was I gonna get out of this mess, for Christ's sake!)

A. T.'s wife Norma is allergic to penicillin. He likes to tell about how she swelled up like a bloated calf once when she got a big dose—and that it was just lucky she was in a hospital at the time or she probably would have died. So I knew this was real serious, that if it *was* a penicillin reaction both me and the cat were in bad trouble. But Fearless wasn't at all swollen up like A. T. says Norma got. Fearless was just limp.

"Hey, don't worry—he's just playin' possum," I said, grasping for straws. "Put him outside and I bet he'll make a run for the barn."

Elaine didn't let on like she was buying that at all. But she did carry her cat out into the yard. Of course Lefty and Domino ran over to smell around on the body and see if maybe they could figure out what all was going on. Elaine locked them up in their pen.

I watched from the kitchen window while Elaine sat in the grass petting the motionless cat. I confess that I was just sick over what had happened, but I didn't want to further upset my wife by acting like I was too concerned. I went out and told her she might as well come on in the house—that the cat would be fine as soon as he saw we were through messing with him.

About thirty minutes later, Elaine hollered at me to come quick.

"He's gone," she said. "Fearless is gone!"

We frantically searched until we found him under an upside-down wheel barrow about twenty feet from where Elaine had left him. I felt a moment of great relief, until I saw that what he'd done was drag himself across the grass by his front legs, and he was so worn out from having done so his tongue was hanging out the side of his mouth. I had to admit that he looked bad, but I tried to sound optimistic by pointing out that at least he had begun to regain the use of two of his legs.

When Elaine couldn't get him to drink some milk that she'd brought outside, she put him on a pillow on the utility porch and sat beside her little cat for the rest of the afternoon and until late that evening. I'd occasionally peek out to see her—tears rolling down her cheeks—rubbing milk on his lips with her finger.

God, I felt just *terrible*.

Later, after Elaine had gone to bed, I went out to check on Fearless one last time. He looked bad—very bad. I hoped he'd be alive in the morning.

He was. It took almost a week before he could run or jump on his usual perches. He looked a lot like he was drunk or suffering from the blind staggers for most of that time—wobbling around, running into things and falling over. A couple of times when Elaine lifted him up on the couch and then forgot to watch out for him, Fearless fell to the floor with a thud.

Looking back, I figure I must have hit a nerve or something when I gave him that penicillin. I guess Elaine forgave me, though. Either that or she's just relieved that Fearless survived. At least she manages to smile good naturedly whenever I casually mention that "I believe it's about time to give Fearless another shot."

TWELVE

A Visit to the Bank

BACK WHEN I TAUGHT SCHOOL, IT WAS
possible—if you got in some kind of financial jam—to borrow
money at bargain basement interest rates through the OU Em-
ployees Credit Union. It was really no big deal. In the morning
you simply filled out a short form asking how long you wanted
the money for and whether you wanted to send your payments
in or have them held out of your paycheck. There was also a
question about the reason you needed the two thousand dollars
or whatever you asked to borrow, but the woman who worked
in the Credit Union office was real helpful and always asked
you that question before you had a chance to write it down so
that if she figured your reason was a little flimsy she could
"suggest" some other lie that she knew the big shots were buying that week. (Like once when I wanted five hundred dollars
to slip down to Acapulco for spring break, she advised me to
put down "Emergency Bypass Surgery.") Usually you picked
your check up that same afternoon.

So when Elaine and I wanted to borrow about eleven hundred dollars to cover a check I'd written for two pairs (that's
four head of cattle: two mother cows and their babies) that we
thought were a bargain at the saleyard, it never occurred to us
that there'd be any problem. After all, Elaine's grandparents had
done business with the local bank since it first opened, and she

had borrowed pretty regularly since taking over the operation of the ranch. Okay, so we had one outstanding note at the time, but it was just about paid up. (Elaine had borrowed to buy a dozen bred heifers back before I even met her.) Hey, *you* watch the news on the television . . . farmers and ranchers are *always* borrowing money. That's just the way things operate in the high-stakes world of American Agri-bidness.

Anyway, we went in as soon as the bank opened the morning after the sale to arrange for a loan. We asked to see the fellow who we'd always done our banking business with, but he was busy or had been laid off or something. The girl at the front desk said would we like to talk with the new vice-president who now handled all the loans?

Sure, we said. Why not? It would be downright un-neighborly to not at least say "Howdy" to the new banker, especially seeing as how he was a vice-president; even though we *did* hate to bother someone so important with such a piddling little loan.

Shaking our hands like he was up for re-election or something, Mr. Vice-President represented himself as fairly palpitating to lend us eleven hundred dollars. He called his secretary over to type out the papers right away so that we could rush back out to Lake Ranch and resume our practice of free enterprise. He offered instant coffee in styrofoam cups and reminisced fondly about his days on his late uncle's dairy farm while we waited for them to print up the money out back.

Pretty soon the secretary appeared with some official-looking papers and a check made out to me. Mr. Vice-President glanced over the document, scribbled his signature on it and then sort of shoved it across the desk for me and Elaine to sign. All the while telling about how once he'd even thought of becoming a dairy farmer himself, but then figured out how he might just enjoy sitting in a fancy air-conditioned office handling large sums of other people's money more than smearing bag balm on chapped udders. The man was a smooth business man, clearly destined to go far in local financial circles.

Now this part right here is embarrassing to me, but I feel obliged to tell it.

We signed the paper. We didn't read it or check for spelling and punctuation or any of the things that common good sense tells a person he ought to do. You know how right above where you sign such documents it says not to sign your name if you don't understand or there are blank places on the paper that might later be filled in? Well that's where we signed it. Right under that warning. We signed up to become the proud borrowers of eleven hundred American dollars at an annual interest rate of 24 percent!

Goddamn it, I watch TV just like you and everybody else in this country. And it just so happened it was the middle of a big presidential campaign right around then and about all the Republican incumbent could talk about was how the interest rates had dropped so much since the GOP had taken up saving the nation that everybody was rich except bankers.

So I said to Mr. Vice-President, "Did I misunderstand you, Mr. Vice-President, or what? Isn't that usury that you're suggesting? Or is it just a get-acquainted joke that new bankers like to tell to break the ice and maybe get a good laugh?"

Mr. Vice-President was immediately taken aback when he heard me say the word *usury,* because it's a word he had only just learned in his second semester in a banking class at the state junior college, but hadn't ever heard anybody actually use before, and had been taught to disavow if he had.

Mr. Vice-President leaned back in his fancy imitation leather chair, put the tips of all his fingers together in front of him, looked real serious, and fell to lecturing me and the wife on how banks all over the country had gone and got themselves in big trouble for having loaned perfectly good money to liberals who just ended up paying it back on time, thus taking all the fun and profit out of the foreclosure business. He added that he had been brought in by the front men (Mr. Marley and Mr. Scrooge?) to be a hard-ass and whip the bank into shape.

He offered to lower the interest rate a point or two if we

would consider increasing the amount of the loan from eleven hundred to, say, at least a half million dollars. Either that, or we could open up a Mini-Jumbo CD and sign it over to him on the spot; then he would loan us *that* money—our own money— at an excellent rate. He sat back and beamed at how reasonable he was.

I allowed as how I didn't really intend to have me a loan at 24 percent; that I'd just hand him back his check to put back in his strongbox or somewhere else real dark, *por favor,* and take my banking business elsewhere.

He said that would be fine, but that if I wanted to pay off my loan *early,* the penalty would be $75 whip-out money. Right *then.* On the spot. (At the time I'd had the loan for about seven minutes.)

I'd like to report I was able to come back with some clever but devastating repartee that humbled and humiliated the sorry bastard in front of a bankful of important customers, or at least divulge that I had a good friend on the Board of Directors who demoted the sumbitch back to drive-in window teller. Unfortunately, I cannot so report.

What I did do was to figure up when the loan of eleven hundred would accrue $75 worth of interest at 24 percent and paid off the note on that day. That and moved our savings account to another bank in another town.

THIRTEEN

Big Red

A LITTLE REMINDER: ELAINE AND I RAISED beef cattle. We did not have milk cows. The two are entirely different beasts altogether. But you probably already knew that.

Okay now, I don't want to gross anybody out, but there's this thing that occasionally happens to a cow that has to do with one of the spigots on her udder getting . . . well, getting *stopped up*. And if it isn't unplugged then it gets all angry and infected and swollen up with sour milk that curdles and . . . well, it's just *nasty*, is what it is. And because it's so nasty, even a calf won't hardly drink from that particular spigot. Then, since not drinking from that one effectively reduces the calf's total available breakfast, lunch, and dinner by roughly twenty-five percent—there being four spigots on the normal udder—the mother cow is likely to raise a smaller and therefore less valuable calf unless the rancher lady who owns the pair can get her new husband to go out and do something about the situation.

No, as a matter of fact, I *don't* know if this happens to milk cows or what dairy farmers do if it does. All I know is that it happened every year to this old Hereford cow that Elaine had when I married her.

Herefords are those red, white-faced cattle that are so popular with everybody in the beef-raising business except Elaine. She had just one—the rest of her cattle were all either Black Angus or Black Brangus or Black Baldies. (She did have one Charolais heifer the first winter we were married. But that particular breed of cattle is cream colored, and I could never find that one when it snowed. So come spring we hauled her to the sale.) Anyway, except for this one Hereford, the rest of our cattle were black. (Okay, if you *must* know there were a lot of times I couldn't find *them* in the snow either, but that's another matter and I don't wish to discuss it.) I never asked, but I suppose it was that Hereford's color that most likely accounts for my wife having named her "Big Red." You remember I told you how Elaine had names for all the cows? Well, Big Red was the first one I learned to identify on sight.

And I remember the first time that I identified her was once when I'd been out on my early morning rounds checking for new babies and escaped bulls and had alertly spotted Big Red's giant udder dragging along behind her in the weeds. Red's calf was about four days old at the time. I went rushing back up to the house hollering for my wife.

"Don't get all excited," Elaine said. "The old biddy did the same thing last year. What we have to do is milk that teat until her baby starts nursing and milking it himself."

Wait a minute, now. I didn't exactly hire on to milk cows, and even *I* knew that folks with good sense didn't generally attempt to milk beef cattle. It's true that our cattle were pretty gentle, but that gentleness didn't seem to extend to actually allowing themselves to be *touched,* much less messed with around their private regions.

But Elaine was already rummaging through the animal medicine chest.

"Here's the milking tubes," she announced.

She held up three needle-like contraptions that looked like the little silver whatchamacallits used to air up volleyballs and basketballs. You know, they look kind of like big hypodermic needles only they have a blunt end and are hollow so that when you stab one into a volleyball you can pump air into it.

Obviously proud to have found them right off, Elaine explained: "You just have to put one of these milking tubes into the plugged teat and drain the milk off . . . you have to do it every twelve hours."

We spent half the day luring Red and her baby down to the pens near the house. I dropped a loop over her head and snubbed her up to a sturdy post. We put some cake down to keep her occupied while I tried to insert one of the tubes into place.

I've already told you about how I used to shoe horses and so had early on learned how quickly and accurately that species can kick a person. Let me tell you that while she may not have the reputation or the reach of a horse when it comes to kicking, a cow is no slouch in that department herself.

Talking to her in a soothing voice the whole time, I gently petted and stroked the cow's flank as I worked my hand down closer to her udder.

"Whoosh!" I heard a funny sound.

"What the hell was that?"

"That was Red's tail," Elaine snickered.

I should point out that Elaine snickered because, as you probably know, some of your less fastidious-type cows have the unsanitary habit of always managing to have a sloppy wet glob of fresh green cowshit smeared around in that big ball of hair on the end of their tails. When Red—one of your less fastidious types—had swished her tail at me, she had succeeded in spraying my clean shirt and hair with a goodly amount of the stuff.

"Whoosh!"

"Well Godamit!" I uncharacteristically whined at my bride. "Can't you at least hold her tail or something?"

"That wasn't her tail," Elaine replied—a little too calmly for my taste, I might add. "She just barely missed kicking your durned head off."

After about thirty minutes, I was finally able to get the tube inserted without getting nailed by a flying foot and I only got hit a few more times with the stinky tail. Then it took another fifteen minutes or so for the milk to drain. We did this twice a day for the next week and a half.

And we did it all again the following calving season, too.

Normally, a cow with a chronic plugged teat isn't worth all the effort—a thrifty cattleperson will just trade her in for a model with good plumbing. But Red raised big old soggy calves and she actually got to the point where she seemed to look forward to her milkings and we kept telling ourselves it wasn't all that much trouble. I don't know, maybe it was because we knew most folks *wouldn't* put up with her.

After we weaned that last calf off of her, though, we hauled Big Red down to the sale in Clovis. She was getting old, like I said, and the fact that it was reasonably clear that she would never get a calf but what she'd need to be milked out for a week or two just sort of made selling her seem like the wise thing to do.

But seeing her down in the auction ring that day was the worst for me as far as selling cattle ever went.

The two guys who operate the gates to let the cows in and out of the ring and then whistle and shout and pop whips to get the animals to turn around and show out for the buyers have probably seen more than their share of rank old cows and sharp-horned steers who'd charge and seriously try to kill or maim them. The ring has welded pipe barricades for those guys to jump behind if things get too hairy, and I've seen many a time when them old boys were more than happy to hide. So it can be dangerous, I know. And I've been to sales where they'll run a couple of thousand head of cattle through the ring in just a few hours. So I understand that those guys can't be expected to recognize a gentle old pet cow everytime they see one—not in that setting, anyway. Still, it was hard as hell to watch Big Red's wide-eyed fear and awful confusion as those two macho cowboy bastards stung her with their whips and hollered—running her this way and that just so the sorry-assed buyer for the dogfood canner could figure how little he wanted to bid.

I don't miss that part of the cow business.

FOURTEEN

Roundup at the Next Ranch Over

YOU MAY HAVE SENSED BY NOW THAT IT'S been my habit for as long as I can remember to prefer the company of those folks who, in polite society at least, are most often referred to as "outlaws." It's like my mother always worried—somewhere along the way I just seem to have fallen in with a bad crowd.

I don't know exactly why that is, except that I guess I've always found them to be more fun to consort with than the bank tellers and notary publics and other big-shot business men and women that I've run across. As a rule, the outlaws I've most enjoyed have been those who, by design or by fate, lead the rugged, rowdy style of life: cowboys and horseshoers, rugby players and college English teachers . . . folks like that.

Which is why when the foreman of a big spread near our place called up one evening to say that he was fixing to ship cattle the following week and wondered if he could count on Elaine and me to help out, I figured it was a good chance to hang out with a bunch of outlaws—that and the fact that helping neighbors work cattle is a part of the tradition in ranch country: an occupational obligation, if you will. I told him we'd be proud to lend a hand.

On the day before the big roundup was scheduled to take place, I lured Rumshop and Moonshine into the corral and

95

nailed a couple of shoes on Rumshop's front feet. Then I trimmed Moonshine's hooves—I didn't shoe *him* . . . there's a limit to how many horses I'll shoe in a given calendar year, and I'd already done one last spring—and knocked some of the dried mud off the both of them. Elaine oiled the saddles while I repeated my lecture on how a horse ought to behave in front of neighbors, and then hooked the trailer to the pickup.

At four o'clock the next morning, it was trying to decide whether to rain or snow as Elaine held a flashlight so that I could see the cinch straps on the saddles. And though they were clearly insulted by the whole affair, the horses eventually allowed me to drag them into the trailer, and we drove on over to the Lazy Z Slash Y Bar Quarter Circle Reverse Seven Headquarters. (I've heard rumors that several smaller steers have died in that outfit's branding pens as a result of third-degree burns over a large portion of their bodies—but that may just be idle gossip.)

We left the horses in the trailer and went inside the foreman's double-wide to drink instant coffee and watch part of an R-rated move on television; it's a big spread and they have one of those fancy satellite dishes that gets about a hundred channels. We were waiting for the rest of the crew to show up.

When about a dozen hands had gathered, the foreman unplugged the TV so that we'd get up off the couch and we all went out and climbed in our rigs to drive in two groups out to where the cattle were rumored to be hiding. Elaine and I ended up following a feed truck supposedly driven by one of the absentee owners of the ranch who'd bussed or flown a bunch of his family and friends out from somewhere or other back east (I think it was Amarillo) to participate in a genuine cattle roundup. I suspect, though, that the truck was really being piloted by some Left Coast tourists who'd taken a wrong turn off the Interstate. I say that because we hadn't gone more than about a hundred yards on a good caliche road when the guy driving the feed truck turned and headed off across a pasture at a high rate of speed like he thought he had the pole position and this was the start of that big off-road race that goes down

Catch Moonshine and the rest will follow (except Comet, of course, who pretends she's not coming).

through the Baja Peninsula in Old Mexico . . . and all the while there were three pickup trucks with horse trailers bouncing along after him like they figured he had good sense! A couple of times we'd come up against a fence or the edge of a deep arroyo and, after turning on their dome light to consult a road atlas and a compass, the tourists in the pace truck would either flip a coin or hold an caucus and vote, and then dash off in another direction.

After about a half hour of this, the feed truck screeched to a halt and a voice from somewhere inside the dust cloud and the black smoke from the burning clutch and brakes announced that we were "there." Elaine and I peered around at dark forms of mesquite and cedar in the pre-dawn light and tried to make out signs of livestock.

We couldn't.

We figured we'd best unload the horses before the crazies inside the truck took a notion to strike out across the plains again.

Now, Elaine maintains that they were just trying to snatch a bite of grass—the horses, that is—and she may be right. But I swear it looked to me like they were kissing the solid ground in gratitude for having survived their wild, bouncing ride in the trailer.

Apparently it was too cold for the five or six folks in the feed truck to leave the warmth of their cab, but they did roll down one window so that they could take pictures while Elaine and I and the three others tightened cinches and mounted our horses.

There we were, five mounted cowpersons hunkered together trying to block off the wind and snow flurries so that the smokers could light matches and the dippers could spit without splattering themselves or a loved one. Talking among ourselves, we came to the realization that we knew only vaguely where we were supposed to be taking the livestock we were supposed to be gathering—and we knew *that* only because one of our group—Calvin Doolittle (not his real name)—admitted that he'd poached deer off this ranch the winter before and reckoned that the headquarters lay somewhere "over yonder." Of course, even if we knew where we were taking them, we still didn't know where they were. We supposed we might be warmer moving, though, so we sort of spread out and set off at a slow lope toward some low hills off to the east.

The tourists, meanwhile, sat comfortably in their warm truck. I imagined them to be sipping steaming mugs of hot coffee laced with Napoleon brandy and nibbling on hot, flaky croissants while they admired the bucolic sight of authentic working cowboys silhouetted against the glorious red of the New Mexico sunrise. . . .

I hoped they'd choke.

We knew that we were out to gather close to a thousand head of yearling steers, and that a convoy of cattle trucks was scheduled to show up at the headquarters stock pens around mid-morning.

We gathered steers for an hour and a half—about six be-

" 'Twas once in the saddle I used to go dashing . . ."

wildered creatures that looked to be as lost as we were—and were trying to push them back in the direction we thought we wanted to go.

Topping a hill, we saw and heard the tourists—merrily honking the horn and scattering feed from the automatic bin mounted on the bed of the truck—surrounded by what appeared to be about six hundred milling steers. Off to the north we could just barely make out the other feed truck—the one that had led the second group of cowboys off earlier that morning. It looked to be leading a couple hundred more steers and maybe a half-dozen folks on horseback.

We spent the next three hours slowly following a herd of already obese steers that would waddle fifty yards or so and then stop to chow down on some more of the feed that the happy folks in the truck were scattering. I thought Elaine was going to

99

cry; we rode our horses over enough feed that morning—scattered and wasted on the ground—to keep our own cattle fat and sleek for at least half the winter.

When we finally managed to get the cattle up to the headquarters, the two feed trucks drove on over to the big house while those of us astride horses worked the bawling animals into the pens. I figured that the folks who'd been in the trucks were probably going back to bed or to watch soap operas beamed down from satellites. I was wrong. Apparently they just needed to reload their cameras and freshen up a bit. The whole bunch was back out to the pens in about fifteen minutes—snapping pictures and hollering stuff like "Yah-Hoo!" and "Ah-Ha!" and referring to the steers as "dogies" (as in "get along little . . .").

The rest of us, like I said, were working the cattle through the pens, counting out twenty head at a time to run across the scales and past the government brand inspector. I was positioned at one end of a long, narrow alley where I could double check the count as the animals passed onto the scales. (I figured I got the job of checking the count by reason of being a college graduate.)

I noticed a middle-aged, highly bejeweled woman in tight-fitting designer jeans and a flowerdy western shirt with mother-of-pearl snaps watching me. She sported a freshly ironed red bandana tied smartly around her neck; a 20X Silver Belly Stetson with a bullrider crease, decorated with a hatband made from the plumage of an endangered species of rare bird, was perched jauntily atop her heavily lacquered platinum blond hairdo. She moseyed over as best she could in her tight jeans and, with some difficulty, climbed up on the "opry seat"—the top rail of the board fence—near where I sat on Rumshop and struck what I imagine she took to be a rodeo queen pose. She'd managed somehow to pick up a big smear of fresh green cow shit on the seat of her brand new designer jeans—the fact of which she was apparently unaware.

At the time, I happened to be between counts and was just

then sticking a big wad of "smokeless tobacco" into my mouth. The lady took my picture with her fancy Nikon camera. I tried to look authentic. It probably would have been better if I'd been lighting up a Marlboro. Real gentleman-like, I offered her a pinch of my Skoal; real lady-like, she declined.

She asked me my name and if I was a "professional" cowboy. It occurred to me then that she just might be a rich, famous photo-journalist on assignment for some slick national magazine, or maybe even preparing one of those fancy picture books on modern-day cowboys.

I propped my leg up over the horn of my saddle picturesquely so that she would be sure and see the new silver spurs Elaine had ordered for me out of the Wards catalog and mumbled words like "Yup" and "Nope" and "Ahh Shucks" in my best affected drawl—addressing the lady as "Ma'am."

As we talked, I began to notice that Elaine and Calvin Doolittle (not his real name)—who had been cutting the steers into bunches of twenty and pushing them down the alley toward me—were having an increasingly difficult time getting the animals to move toward my end. Later on we figured out that the heavy smell of the lady's French perfume was probably boogering the steers—them being Mexican by birth and so not used to high-toned European odors. At least when she climbed down off the fence and wandered on over to where the state inspector was checking brands, the steers calmed down and it was the government man who started acting boogered.

Other than that, though, the sorting and loading went pretty well. When the last cattle truck pulled out onto the highway, somebody startled me and most of the horses by clanging a big bell over by the main house. A rather portly gentleman dressed casually, yet smartly, in what I took to be clothes ordered directly from the L. L. Bean catalog came over and announced that if we'd leave our horses in one of the pens and wash some of the stink off at the garden hose over by the side of the house, we were all invited in for what he called "grub." I halfway expected we'd find a bearded old-timer named Cookie serving up

End of a long day

slumgullion from a chuck wagon in the front yard and the Sons of the Pioneers singing melodious tunes from the shady veranda.

The fellow in the L. L. Bean britches sat at the head of a long table where the dozen of us ate from paper plates heaped full of barbecued beef and beans and drank iced tea. The tourists stood around the table and watched us eat. I don't know about those others, but it made *me* feel real popular. I mean, I figured they were going to go back to wherever they were from and tell their neighbors that they had watched real cowboys eat dinner. Shucks, their children might even go back to boarding school and write "What I did on my summer vacation" themes about it. Nobody asked for my autograph, but they were probably just too nervous to approach me.

As soon as we'd finished eating, a young man I hadn't noticed before drove us and Calvin Doolittle (not his real name) out into the pasture to look for our pickups and trailers. It took awhile, but we finally found them.

Elaine and I loaded Rumshop and Moonshine and drove on home. It had been a long, dusty day—and we still had our own cows to feed and some fence to mend.

FIFTEEN

On Civic Responsibility

I'LL ADMIT THAT I'M NOT MUCH OF A joiner when it comes to service organizations and fraternal orders and things like that.

I've got a friend who's a high sheriff down at the local Brotherhood or Order of something or other for the Greater Santa Rosa area. He went through a spell where he was by-god determined he was going to get me to leave my unsavory past behind and to memorize the prescribed ritual and learn the secret handshake, and become a ring-wearing member. I tried to tell him that he and the others didn't really want someone like me in their secret conclave, but he kept the pressure up for a while. Maybe they were having a big membership drive and he was in line to win a toaster or something if he recruited enough new folks. He hasn't mentioned it for a long time, so I figure they must have filled their quota.

Listen, I went to college in the 1960s, that decade when college students were inclined to demonstrate against things and to practice free speech by talking rude and ugly about bankers and other clean-shaven businessmen. And while it's true I worked my way up to big-shot cattle baron, it's also a fact that the good folks who were my neighbors in Santa Rosa looked at the world from a vastly different perspective than I.

For example, most of them would openly admit that they not

only voted for Ronald ("*Rambo*") Reagan *twice!*—but for
Richard ("I Am Not a Crook") Nixon, as well. I have it on
good authority that there are among them dues-paying members of the Moral Majority, the Masons, the Farm Bureau, the
CowBelles, and, for all I know, the DAR and the PTA. They
consider a good many of the folks I admire to be pointy-headed
liberals, if not actual communist sympathizers; and for reasons I
can't explain, they either didn't count me among them or else
felt sorry enough for Elaine that they chose to overlook that
flaw in my character. My hair was maybe a bit too long for
their tastes, but then I usually had a respectable amount of cow
manure on my boots, and my knuckles were generally pretty
banged up from doing manual labor. Too, I'd often been observed chewing tobacco in public.

These are good folks I'm talking about. They were my
friends. I just wanted to point out some of the differences between me and my fellow citizens in Guadalupe County so that
you might better understand what I'm about to tell you.

On Christmas Eve I got a letter from the office of the
County Clerk in Santa Rosa. I figured it was probably a
Christmas card or maybe a note of congratulations for having
been the only registered voter in the entire county to have cast
100 percent of his votes for losers in the previous month's elec-
tions, so I didn't get too excited.

It was a greeting all right—a summons to appear for jury
duty and a threat that failure to appear carried a lengthy jail
term with a diet of dry tortillas and tap water.

Stapled to the summons was a questionnaire that I was directed to fill out and bring with me when I reported for active
duty in early January. There were questions like, *Do you have
any living relatives who are law enforcers?* and *Do you want to be
excused from jury duty?*

I admitted in writing that my brother had dropped out of the
Ph.D. program at the University of Oklahoma in favor of becoming a cop, and that both my sister and my daughter are
Deputy United States Marshals. While brother Chris keeps a
watchful eye out for evil-doers in the greater Oklahoma City

You're right . . . a wreck is about to happen

area, sister Ann and child Isabel kick down doors looking for tax-evading drug dealers and godless communists in Alabama. (They might be pulling my leg, but they tell me that the commies are readily distinguished from the natives by their unAmerican preference for Russian borscht over Alabama *bobbycue—Roll Tide!*) All of which was solid enough evidence, I believed, to establish I was from a long line of gun-toting rednecks who would jump up and yell "Guilty!" at a minority group member or a longhair at the drop of a gavel. Therefore anyone with Querry family genes was clearly unfit to sit in impartial judgment of any citizen of these United States. Just to be on the safe side, though, I answered the other question that, Yes, I'd very much like to be excused from jury duty owing to the fact that not being able to check on my cows several times a day would prove to be an insufferable hardship on me—not to mention the effect it would have on my sickly wife—and might possibly even prevent me from sending in my regular monthly contributions to the ACLU and the SPCA.

On the appointed day, I drove into town and found a parking place in front of the county courthouse and went in to whine and gnash my teeth while pleading poverty and/or moral turpitude—whatever it took to get out of courtroom duty for the next six months. Me and about two hundred other citizens.

After turning our questionnaires and excuses over to the clerk, we were all herded into the courtroom. After about an hour, somebody hollered for us all to stand up, and then the judge came in and welcomed us all like we were the most patriotic group of individuals he'd ever had the privilege to know. To hear him tell it, everyone else in the entire county was derelict if not downright un-American for not having shown up that morning, even though they hadn't been called. He allowed as how he was sure none of us model citizens would even *think* of asking to be excused from our civic obligation unless, of course, we were scheduled to report to the Humana Hospital in Louisville in the next day or so to have our new artificial heart hooked up. I mean, this guy made Judge Joseph Wopner of "The People's Court" look almost smart. (Or am I the only one in America who thinks Wopner is a jerk?)

Anyway, after we'd all laughed respectfully at his clever wit, this judge got real serious and asked for a show of hands of all those convicted felons among us whom, according to the law, he was obliged to excuse. That thinned us out pretty good, right there. Then he went on to confess he had a soft spot in his heart for teachers of little children and volunteer church workers, and with a wave of his black-robed arm excused all the members of those noble occupations. Again, a good number of people hurried for the door.

With that, the judge solemnly bestowed upon the fifty or so of us remaining the high honor and respected title of qualified jurors and, after making us stand up and promise to uphold the constitution of the sovereign state of New Mexico, congratulated us once again for being such truly fine Americans.

After a fifteen-minute recess—during which we were cautioned not to leave the room—the clerk and the bailiff carried in a wire cage filled with small slips of folded-up paper. (Like the guy used to use to draw the lucky phone number on "Dialing for Dollars.") The judge called us back to order, and told the clerk to proceed with the drawing.

I didn't exactly know what was going on, but I figured we weren't fixing to take part in a raffle for a new Buick or for dinner for two down at the Dairy Queen, and I hadn't noticed anybody handing out Bingo cards, so I just sat quietly. When my name was the first one drawn, I stifled the impulse to rush forward to claim my prize. There were some recidivist jurors in the room; and you could tell by the audible sigh of relief that went up when *my* name was drawn that "winning" was not the best thing that could happen. Sure enough, I learned later that the drawing had been to determine the order in which those qualified would be called upon to serve.

Once all of us had been drawn into our respective order of preference, the judge fairly beamed as he announced we were especially fortunate in that there was at that very moment, waiting in the wings, a local gentleman who stood accused of selling and distributing a green, leafy substance the police did not think was alfalfa. In short, we had been summoned, questioned, qualified, and rated—now we were going to serve.

The judge directed the bailiff to escort the accused into the courtroom. Then—and I must say I found this most peculiar— the judge introduced us to everybody in the room. First the assistant district attorney who would prosecute the case on behalf of the citizens of the state of New Mexico, then the counsel for the defense, and finally, the accused. I was struck by how much it was like the start of the World Series or the Super Bowl—I kept waiting for the defense lawyer and the guy on trial to jump up and give each other a "high five," or at least to pat one another on the butt.

Once we were all well acquainted, the D.A. took the first turn at questioning the prospective jurors again.

He asked, Did we know the accused? (Easily a third of the group indicated they did, although no one within my hearing owned up to having ever bought their dope from him.) Did anyone know the defense lawyer? (A pretty silly question, I thought, seeing as how few people will admit publicly to knowing a lawyer personally. No hands were raised.) The D.A. named off the witnesses he was going to call to testify against the guy and asked if any of us knew them. About a dozen hands went up, but the judge only excused those seven or eight who claimed they were actually related to the witnesses. I considered admitting to being somebody's brother-in-law in a last-ditch effort at getting excused, but I chickened out when it occurred to me that the judge might see that I was lying and send me off to the penitentiary for impersonating a relative.

By the time the defense lawyer had his turn at grilling the jury, it looked like there were only about two of us in the room who weren't related to—or living with someone who was related to—the guy on trial or one of the witnesses . . . those two being me and the bailiff. Now, I may not have attended law school, but I'd seen enough old "Perry Mason" reruns to know that what we had here was a situation where they'd have to move this trial to another county—if not another state—and I would soon be on my way home.

But the judge warned us again about leaving the room, and he and the lawyers went out to hold a meeting.

Pretty soon the bailiff shouted at us to stand up again, and the judge reappeared. He gave us an emotional speech about how sorry he was that only twelve of us could be lucky enough to hear this poor fellow's case and begged those not selected not to take it personal and get all depressed. Then he read off the names of the twelve lucky jurors (mine, of course, was first), and the bailiff directed us to our chairs in the jury box.

Everybody else got to go home. I spent the better part of the next two days at the courthouse.

I learned some things about the legal system in those two days that I'd only guessed at before. Things like how the presiding judge won't allow members of the jury to take notes. I guess they must've had a lot of people just sit up there and doo-

dle or something, but I'd sure have felt better if I'd been able to
take notes. And learned just how little truth there seems to be
to what anybody says in a courtroom even though they've been
sworn to tell it whole and nothing but.

For instance, I listened to the defendant carefully relate a conversation that transpired between him and the sheriff. And then
the sheriff was called in to give his side of the story and I listened to him recall something completely different—I mean,
not even *close*. Of course you're probably thinking that the defendant in a felony case isn't exactly what you'd call your most
reliable witness. But listen. . . . Then they called up a third
party—an intelligent-enough-looking deputy sheriff who allowed as how he was personally present during the alleged conversation—who swore that the conversation he was witness to
didn't even slightly resemble what either of the previous two
guys recounted. Now, I'm aware of course, that the whole reason for having the traditional twelve-person jury made up of
red-blooded American freedom-fighters is that supposedly in
their collective wisdom it will be immaculately revealed to them
exactly what is the TRUTH. I am not, however, persuaded that
such a revelation is likely to occur.

I'm not going to go into all the testimony and the evidence
that was presented, because it was routine and relatively boring.
Besides, all that stuff's a matter of public record and if you're
fairly palpitating to know all the details of the case, you can just
go down to the Guadalupe County Courthouse and look it up
yourself. What I will relate here is a little of what all went on
behind the locked doors of the jury room.

After giving us another of his lectures—this time on how he
wanted us to just forget a bunch of the stuff that went on the
courtroom—the judge read us some directions on what all we
were allowed to consider in reaching our verdict in the case.
For example, he said we could consider only what we'd heard
in the courtroom and nothing else. Then he had the bailiff lock
us all up in a tiny little room with an aluminum coffee pot. We
were supposed to knock on the door real loud when we reached
our verdict.

I guess most of the jurors knew each other pretty well already, because they immediately started asking one another about how much rain had the other gotten lately and how was old Uncle Joe getting along since his stroke? . . . stuff like that. I recognized one woman because she was a part-time checker over at the grocery store, but I'd never before seen any of the others as near as I could recall. Finally, after listening to these folks chat among themselves for about fifteen minutes I cleared my throat and asked if maybe we shouldn't get down to the business at hand . . . that I didn't know about any of them, but I personally needed to get on home and count my cows.

At that everybody acted stunned and confused . . . like they didn't know they were there to conduct any kind of business and didn't really have any idea of what was expected of them. I boldly suggested that maybe we ought to take a quick survey to see if by chance we were unanimous in our feelings about the guy on trial because if so we could commence to knocking on the door to signal the judge that everything was taken care of. They all grinned and acted like they thought that was a real good idea and suggested that since I had come up with such a crackerjack plan right off the top of my head, why didn't I just go on and take over as the foreman of this jury. I thanked them kindly for the high honor, and asked for a show of hands of those who wanted to find the guy guilty. Seven hands went up.

Since we were so obviously split, I carefully (and, I'll admit, dramatically) read aloud the instructions the judge had given us, stressing the part about "beyond a shadow of a doubt." Then I explained how even though I personally suspected the defendant probably was a small-time crook and that he was likely even guilty of dealing dope now and then, I still felt obliged to follow the instructions given to us by the judge. And if I was going to follow those instructions, I had to admit to having a shadow of a doubt mainly owing to the fact that the sheriff and his deputy hadn't even exhibited the common sense to get their stories straight before they were called up to testify.

One of the jurors who'd raised his hand during the guilty

vote—and who, I discovered later, had been personally called to witness in the Big Trial of Life as a street preacher—interrupted me right about then.

"All I know is that the guy sells marijuana and probably a lot of other dangerous narcotics. *Ever'*body knows that our children are being poisoned by these devil worshipers."

The fellow sitting next to the street preacher nodded in agreement and mumbled.

"Amen . . . Thank You, Jesus!"

Again, I read aloud the judge's instructions. Only this time I stressed the part about how we were to consider only the testimony and evidence presented in the court. Then I called for another vote. This time the count was ten to two for acquittal.

Trust me, you really don't want me to relate the conversations that went on during the next five hours we spent in the jury room. Suffice it to say that the preacher and his disciple sidekick at one point actually suggested that we all kneel together in prayer for Divine guidance on whether or not we should petition the judge to give that sinful dope-dealing communist in the other room the electric chair—in Jesus' name, of course.

I sent a note out to the judge telling him that we were deadlocked. He sent the bailiff to fetch us some hamburgers and fries and instructed us to keep trying—that he was sure such a fine jury as he knew in his heart we were could resolve any question with a little time and a free Big Mac. Apparently he thought we were just acting cranky because we were hungry.

I'll say one thing, the two holdouts never once faltered in their convictions. Oh sure, they did admit candidly that even *they* didn't think the D.A. had proven that the guy was guilty. But they insisted that that didn't make any difference at all . . . that they were certain that the guy must have done *something* and so it was their Christian duty to send the scumball to jail.

I sent another note out to the judge telling him it was truly hopeless. He called everybody back into the courtroom and lectured us awhile and then polled the jurors one at a time—to be sure the foreman wasn't just trying to pull a fast one, I guess. Then he thanked us sincerely on behalf of the governor and all the other good folks in the state and we were excused.

I never did hear if the D.A. re-tried the guy. If he did, I know I wasn't invited to be on the jury.

SIXTEEN

High Society, Santa Rosa–Style

MY FRIEND A. T. DOES HIS BEST THINKING
and joke making-up when he's riding around on his big green
John Deere tractor down in what he likes to call his wheat field.
Lots of times he'll make up stories and hold conversations with
himself on some imagined person. It's just a real creative time
for him.

I remember one time he was telling me about how he had
been riding around on his tractor thinking about rich people
who drive Mercedes automobiles and play golf and polo and
spend a lot of time at country clubs. Apparently that led to him
studying on what all the whole idea of a country club involved.
And from there he went on to work out a plan about how he
wanted to start up a "City Club"—for folks who already live
out in the country and want to do city things.

He figured he'd need to rent a building in town—right on the
main street, if possible—for this club. Members (and only dead
serious Republican church-goers with Anglo surnames could
even qualify to *apply* to become members, and even then they'd
probably just be put on a waiting list) could come in and do to
the city what city folks go out to do to the country.

For instance, City Club members could bring old mattresses
and sofas and blown-out tires into town as often as once a week
and dump them out on the curb or in somebody's front yard;

115

Ron caking from the pickup

or at the very least they could drive their pickups around and toss beer cans and disposable diapers out in the streets. And of course City Club members could bring their guns with them whenever they came into town and go hunting in city folks' yards, leave their gates open, shoot holes in their mailboxes and in street signs, and sometimes even accidentally shoot city animals: dogs, cats, parakeets . . . whatever. Just good clean city fun.

What got me thinking about A. T.'s idea for a City Club was that Elaine and I got invited to formally join the Santa Rosa social scene. I know I told you earlier that Santa Rosa has a Holiday Inn, and a Stuckeys, and a Truckstops of America and not a whole lot else. What I didn't tell you was—now hold on to your hats—it also has a Country Club!

Even though I'm not above doing so, I'm not making this up. They really do call this place a Country Club and there's

Elaine and her grandfather caking from the pickup about twenty-five years earlier

not one bit of irony in their voices when they do so. It's actually just a cinderblock building that resembles a medium-sized milking barn as much as anything. This lone building sits up on a little rise overlooking a small lake—more like a pond—with one shade tree and a couple of picnic tables and a combination boat/fishing/sunbathing dock floating around on old fifty-gallon oil drums. They get along without the traditional golf course and polo field. It's about a half-mile out of town—on the road toward Puerto de Luna. There isn't a sign or a pair of those red-lipped Negro lawn jockey statues or anything like that to show you where to turn off the pavement, but you can check with them down at the feedstore for directions. I guess the board of directors at the club figures that if they were to put up a sign of some kind announcing the existence of such a ritzy and exclusive place, all kinds of undesirables might try to join up, even though the dues are kind of steep at forty bucks a year, up front!

The way that Elaine and I got involved is, we were invited by the insurance agent's wife to attend a pot-luck dinner and she said it was going to be held at the Country Club.

At first, we were disinclined to go, neither of us ever having been there before and not knowing whether we even had the proper attire. But then we decided, what the heck . . . if we ever wanted to have any social life at all, we'd better get it in gear and start attending events other than livestock auctions and calf brandings. Up until then we'd only been to one social event where your clothes stayed clean, and that was the time we went to a Farm Bureau meeting at the Adobe Inn Cafe Banquet Room just before Christmas. The scary thing to me was that when the lady called up Elaine with the invitation to the Country Club, she mentioned that after everybody ate, they usually played games.

I didn't know if we should be prepared for touch football or ice hockey or what. The last time I'd been at a gathering where they'd played any kind of games was an impromptu get together of the rugby team in Norman. And *that* had been little more than just a regular team meeting with lots of Mexican polio weed getting passed around.

I was pretty sure those weren't the kind of games they were likely to play at the Santa Rosa Country Club. But I doubted there would be the facilities for bowling, so I didn't wear my Panther City Methadone Center League bowling shirt with my name over the pocket that I'd received as a door prize from the lawyer Kirk Purcell at "Walk Tall America Night" in Fort Worth, Texas. Instead I wore clean Levis and a regular shirt. Elaine made a kind of a creamy casserole dish out of green beans and nuts. I was surprised at the large turnout. All the men kept to one side of the room, talking about measurable precipitation and cattle prices while the women busied themselves around the long tables with "SRCC" stenciled on them (just like those tables they used to have in your high school cafeteria), uncovering the covered dishes and trying to keep the children who were running and screaming around the room

Elaine and Ron

from using their fingers to dig all the chocolate icing off the big sheet cake.

There were some of the folks there who'd helped out with the big roundup over at the Lazy Z Slash Y Bar Quarter Circle Reverse Seven, and of course the insurance agent who also sold the blackleg vaccine was there, and even that usurious bastard from the bank who I'd have supposed spent all his free time down in the basement of his house figuring up amortization schedules and practicing his foreclosure laugh. There was a

Methodist preacher—not the one who works as a mail carrier, but another one.

Everyone got to eat all they wanted after the Methodist preacher got up and tried to say a prayer over the screaming noise of the children. I especially liked the fact that there were about a dozen different desserts—not counting what was left of the sheet cake that the children had dug up—and it seemed to be okay if you took some of each kind.

When everyone had cleaned their plates, some of the women, in the tradition of rural women-folk, started clearing off the tables. The men lit up pipes and cigars and whipped out tins of snuff and pouches and plugs of chewing tobacco. I noticed that there were two-pound coffee cans placed strategically here and there for use as spittoons, something I had never before noticed in a country club.

Then one of the women who acted like she might be an important office-holder in the Club, or maybe the Immediate Past President or something, came around and asked everybody what was their pleasure in the game department. . . .

"Here it comes," I whispered to Elaine. "I'll bet you a dollar bill this bunch'll vote for charades."

Instead, the woman passed around a couple of decks of playing cards and a box of dominoes and a Trivial Pursuit game.

The men grabbed up the dominoes and one deck of cards and got off by themselves to play men-type games and probably tell off-color jokes and cuss. About a half-dozen of the women stayed over by the big aluminum coffee pot where they could check on the caffeine supply and still keep an eye on the rowdy children. The rest of the women split up and either played canasta or Trivial Pursuit.

I guess I just don't really understand why is it that there are men-type games, anyway. And I'm not just talking here about National League Football, either; I can at least see the point of those folks who don't think the sexes should be all mixed up out on the plastic grass of the Superdome. No, I'm talking about the less violent, more social kinds of games. Like checkers. When was the last time you saw two old women sitting on park benches playing checkers? Or watched a re-run of "The Waltons" where they showed a group of ladies gathered in Ike's General Store sitting around chewing tobacco and playing dominoes? And I figure about the only time you're likely to see a female playing the manly game of poker is on some TV comedy show, and then it's usually meant to make fun of either the woman who's playing or the men she's beating—the laughs come when we see that she's good at a traditional male-bonding game.

And of course, it's not just games I'm talking about. I get the idea roles that folks feel comfortable with are much more rigidly defined among New Mexico ranchland inhabitants than they are among your Eastern liberals in, say, New Hampshire.

You may not believe this, but the Women's Movement has not yet reached Santa Rosa, New Mexico. For example, hair dressers, school teachers, and book authors there are all considered to be engaged in "women's work"—and I suspect such is the case in most all of the rural Southwest.

"Now wait just a durned minute," you're probably saying. "If that's the case, then how come those same folks didn't think Miss Elaine was a little, shall we say, *strange* for running that ranch all by herself before you came along to help out?"

Okay, if you must know, I believe they probably did . . . that the few women with whom Elaine came in contact back then were certainly taken aback, and maybe just a little bit jealous, to see that she did all the things on her ranch that it took their husbands, hired hands, and burly sons to do on theirs. And I suspect they may have even felt a little sorry for Elaine for not having caught herself a man back in junior high school like most of them had. Why, everybody knows that only professional rodeo queens are unmarried past the age of sixteen—and then only because beauty queens are too busy performing royal duties and thinking about glamorous careers to worry over gettin' married until they're at least twenty.

I don't suppose I should've been surprised to learn that one of the things that Elaine could always count on whenever she saw any of the local ladies after we got married was the burning

Matchmaker (Josie's first foal) and Moonshine

question about when she was going to stop working like a man and start having babies? I honestly believe that it was beyond their comprehension that any woman would actually choose to do something other than cook, keep house, and raise children.

I think that the men, on the other hand, admired Elaine's gumption in taking on the ranch and the cattle single-handedly. But, seeing as how she was generally a good head taller than most of them, anyway, I'm sure they must've figured it was a cryin' shame that such an otherwise pretty young girl was des-tined for old maidhood just because she preferred raising dogied calves to having babies like the good Lord intended womenfolk to do—besides which, she was so dad-burned *tall*.

I never did learn to play dominoes, or poker, or any of those other traditional male-bonding games; they've never been very appealing to me ever since I was in the service and would see guys lose all their pay in a single sitting. Besides, if the truth be known, I always preferred to bond with the ladies, anyway.

That evening at the country club I ended up having a real fine time playing Trivial Pursuit with Elaine and the preacher's wife and a handful of other women. The women had a lot more to talk about than the men. I worried for a few days that I might not be thought of as one of the guys. And I'll admit it was important to me at the time that I be viewed as a top hand—what my neighbors might call a good ol' boy—if only because I knew folks were right fond of my wife and were watching closely to see what this outsider that she'd married was like. I don't know, maybe I should have learned to play dominoes. It's just that playing dominoes or checkers has always seemed to me like something old men do. It's not that I was uncomfortable trying to answer questions about The Beaver and Wally Cleaver; hell, I was pretty good at it. But Trivial Pursuit isn't what you'd call "manly," and you won't be surprised to learn that they attach a lot of importance to macho-ness in that part of the country.

We didn't get invited back to any more functions at the Club right away, and so I assumed we'd made a bad impression. But then a couple of months later we got a letter from the president of the Club.

Dear Ron and Elaine,
The members of the Country Club are pleased to inform you that your name has been approved, by the Screening Committee, for Club membership. . . .
The dues are forty-five dollars and are payable to "The Santa Rosa Country Club." Juanita June Scroggins, down at the Gas Company, has been kind enough again this year to be in charge of collecting the dues and will issue a dues card and keys to the gate, as the locks have already been changed.
Yes, we are planning to have a year book and as soon as they are ready, they will be passed out to the membership.

I must tell you that even though we did pass the careful scrutiny of the Screening Committee, Elaine and I never officially joined up. To be honest, I think the dues having gone up to forty-five dollars might just have put it out of our reach. I've bought *cars* for less money.

SEVENTEEN

Comet

ONE OF MY FAVORITE PHOTOGRAPHS SITS
on a dresser in our back bedroom. It's a small, faded color
snapshot of a little girl, five or six years old, sitting bareback
astride a young horse. Beside her stands a tall man in a straw
hat and blue work shirt; he's smiling at the girl. In one hand the
man holds the knotted lead rope attached to the horse's halter,
with the other he reassuringly steadies the young rider. The girl
and the horse are looking toward the camera. She is clutching
one hand tightly to the horse's mane, her other hand is on the
man's shoulder.

The little girl in the photograph is my wife. The man is her
grandfather. The horse is Comet.

Mind you, that picture was taken on the ranch more than
twenty-five years before I knew Elaine—or Comet. By the time
I met her, she had become a grouchy old woman. (The horse,
that is, not my wife.)

During the time I knew her, and for some years before,
Comet was the boss of all the horse critters on Lake Ranch. It
was as simple as that. Comet just naturally felt it her duty in
life to keep the ranch horses in line, especially the youngsters.
(You can just forget all that stuff you've been taught at the picture show and in books about how the handsome shining black
stallion lords it over his band of mares and young colts and

Elaine on Comet beside her grandfather

fillies. The fact of the matter is, it's really some grouchy older
female in the bunch that runs the show. You know, just like in
real life.)

Comet was what the horsey set would refer to as "a push-
button ride." By that, I mean that it was safe to put visiting city
slickers and obnoxious little children up on her. She'd generally
look mad and lay her ears back and sigh a lot, but she wouldn't
run away with them, or buck, or otherwise act in a dangerous

Elaine on Comet beside her grandfather

manner. I figure the reason Comet didn't do any of these things
was mainly because she thought since folks were always cluck-
ing at her or shouting "giddy-up" and kicking their heels into
her sides, that they wanted her to run or at least to trot—and
she was far too grouchy to do what she thought anybody
wanted her to do.

Comet had this habit of going dead lame whenever someone
climbed up on her old swayed back for a leisurely stroll out
across the pasture. Of course the minute we'd take off her saddle and turn her out, she'd tear off running and kicking her
heels up as though she were once again the young filly in the
photograph.

And I remember that whenever Elaine and I would saddle up
Rumshop and Moonshine to move cows from one pasture to
another or to gather up some calves we wanted to work, we'd
generally let Comet come along. She knew the cattle business

from her twenty years of working with Elaine's grandfather and I swear she understood what all was going on. Only rarely did she ever get in the way—she was usually a help, in fact.

When Elaine and I moved off the ranch, we naturally intended to take care of the old mare. Elaine had practically grown up with Comet, and besides, she had been the last horse that my wife's grandfather—who was known far and wide as one hell of a horseman—had broken to ride. That alone should assure a dignified retirement. As likely as not we'd have simply moved Comet to our new place along with our other horses who she knew and loved to boss around.

On the other hand, if—when the time came for the big move—Comet had seemed the least bit sickly or looked at all poor, I suspect I would have taken her down by the north well—out to one of the grassy spots she loved so—and put her down. She was, after all, uncommonly long lived for a horse, and as far as Elaine knew she'd never once been off the six thousand acres that made up Lake Ranch. Relocating and adjusting to another part of the country might well have proven too difficult for the old thing.

I'm ashamed to tell you we left the old mare there on the ranch when we moved off. Winter was approaching and she was out there all alone. Horses are among the most sociable of animals, and we left Comet there by herself . . . there were no people, no livestock, no nothing.

We didn't think that was what we were doing. We thought she was going to be taken care of. You see, the big shots who had finagled fiduciary control of Lake Ranch back when Elaine's grandfather died—and therefore of Comet, who was and always had been a part of the ranch—decided that if Elaine was going so much out of her way to take the old mare with her, it must be because she was worth a trainload of money—at least to Elaine—and by-god they weren't about to take a chance on missing out on a dollar. Anyway, these jerks had their big-deal lawyer send Elaine a letter saying that if she wanted to remove Comet from the ranch, she'd have to *buy* the old mare from

The old mare, Comet

them, and named a ridiculously high price! Remember now, these good people lived off in the suburbs of some fairly good-sized city, so it's not as though they had any interest in taking my wife's old pal into their own lives, or that they would have had the slightest notion of how to care for her if they had.

I'm not able to tell you what happened to Comet. We were led to believe she was going to be sold, and while we hoped she'd go to someone with some sense, reason told us she'd probably end up at a packing plant. We learned later from the fellow who had the place next to Lake Ranch that these folks who were going to take over running things so well had just left the old mare there that winter—that he would occasionally see her walking the fence line when he was feeding cows. He said he'd felt sorry for her and sometimes thrown her a chunk of hay and had broken ice so she could drink at the stock tank.

No, he didn't call us up at the time and let us know she was being neglected. I don't know why; maybe he didn't think it was any of his business. Maybe Comet made it through the winter. Maybe she got hauled over to the killer in Tucumcari. Maybe. . . .

I can tell you that to this day I deeply regret the fact that I did not shoot Comet the morning we left Lake Ranch. It would have been the kinder thing to do.

EIGHTEEN

Beat the Drum Slowly

I FIGURE THE BIG QUESTION IN EVERY-
one's mind is, So why did you guys ever leave the ranch, anyway? I mean, why in the world would anyone sell all their pet
cows and move up north to Taos just because that's where
there's green trees and tourists from Texas who test drive their
Winnebagos around the town plaza all day?

Okay, so I'm sure it sounds to you like we were having ourselves a real big time there on Lake Ranch. And I know I told
you how the place had been home and even provided a meager
income for Elaine's grandparents and for her great-grandparents
before them ever since it was first homesteaded back in whenever it was. And it doesn't take a whole lot of figuring to see
that Elaine flat out loved the place—that she'd brought a greenhorn like me on board only when it looked like she'd be able to
mold me into at least a passable hand, and then only after she'd
made clear in no uncertain terms that she intended to spend the
rest of her life there on that ranch, and that if I had notions of
living elsewhere I would by-god have to do so with somebody
besides her. We had a nice bunch of good cattle that were the
envy of Guadalupe County. Why, we'd even been invited to
join the local country club.

But Elaine didn't get to live out her life on her ranch. And
we didn't join the Country Club. No, we sold our good cattle

to a young couple just starting out in ranching, turned our horses out on a friend's pasture, packed up all our personal belongings, loaded Lefty and Domino and the cats into a borrowed car, and moved about a hundred miles north to a seventy-five-year-old adobe house at the foot of Taos Mountain. And like I said, you're probably wondering why.

A short time before he passed away, Elaine's grandfather had a will and a trust document drawn up with a big-city bank wherein he ultimately left his beloved ranch in undivided interest to his only heirs—Elaine being the youngest among them. While I'm persuaded that it never seriously entered his mind that anyone with Bibb blood in their veins would consider selling the property, I figure he left the ranch in *undivided* shares as a kind of insurance so that no single heir could sell his or her part. Too, I'm certain it was obvious to him that, with one exception, these heirs had neither the desire nor the skill to operate or even live on a working cattle ranch. As the old man had told one of his nieces over in Albuquerque shortly before he died, "The baby knows how to run the place—I taught her, and she knows." The baby to whom he referred was Elaine.

And he was right. Elaine *did* know how to run the ranch. But first she had to make the place into a working cow outfit. When she moved onto the ranch a couple of months after her grandfather's funeral, the only livestock in residence was the old mare Comet and a sizable community of rattlesnakes and coyotes. Elaine went out and borrowed a good cow horse, propped up some of the worst stretches of fence, and began buying a few cattle at auctions. She studied hard and worked out a plan that, with a little luck and a good deal of hard work on her part, she figured would cause the place to become self-supporting within five years. (There was no mortgage on the place, and the taxes were less than $400 a year.) In return for her full-time labor, Elaine was to receive room and board and a small salary. I probably don't have to tell you that when you're the only hand on a working cow-calf operation, "full-time" means exactly that—there's no such thing as a day off. For ex-

ample, it's still difficult for me to conjure up the picture of
Elaine spending the Christmas Eve before I met her sitting up
alone with a heifer calf she'd pulled a few days earlier whose
mother had died. Yeah, I know that a lot of us have spent some
holidays alone—but still, that doesn't make it any easier for me
to recall.

I guess you could say that for Elaine, working the ranch was
clearly a labor of love. I don't think she ever truly cared much
one way or the other about the money she was paid. In fact,
the bookkeeper for the ranch account was actually paid a larger
salary than Elaine got.

Anyway, I don't really intend to go into all the reasons Elaine
and I moved off the ranch, because it still makes me mad. My
wife is a calm and a gentle woman; she works hard at avoiding
conflict of any sort—a good and enviable character trait, to be
sure. But as such, it's clear to me that she put up with a lot of
needless crap for a good many years. And she did so mostly, I
think, because she was all alone in having taken on the awe-
some responsibility of her grandfather's ranch and of the animals, and she needed her energy for more important things
than dealing with the silly, self-serving notions of ignorant city
slickers.

When we were married, Elaine—for the first time, I believe—came to be viewed by the "significant other" in her life
as something other than a child. My wife began to see herself
mirrored in the way I saw her—that is, as the mature and
knowledgeable cattle rancher that she really was. It's true a lot
of folks in similar circumstances would continue to view such a
life on a ranch through the eyes of the child: which is to say as
though they would always be just kids playing cowboys and Indians on a summer weekend at Grandpa's ranch—fishing and
swimming in stock tanks, riding horses, having picnics, and
taking long naps. In short, some of your more unreasonable
types might just think Elaine was having too durned much fun.
Why, them old cows just walked around and ate grass all
day . . . *anybody* could see that. Never mind that the ranch had
started to turn a profit, Elaine had married and seemed just a

little too happy for some folks' tastes. Besides, like one occasional female visitor complained, she didn't like the idea of having to close the door when she went to the bathroom now that Elaine had a husband living in the house.

But I said I wasn't going to go into all of this. I'm willing to admit to being a troublemaker—one who does not suffer fools gladly. Suffice it to say that some of the folks involved in the trust got together and outvoted Elaine and then figured out they'd sell the jointly owned cattle and while they were at it, everything else on the place as well—the pickup, the trailer, the extra half-rolls of barbed wire, the squeeze chute . . . everything down to the furnishings in the house! And of course then they figured Elaine should probably no longer draw wages for working the ranch, either—it being unstocked, and unfurnished, and all. (I'll point out that for the two years I was on the ranch I was never paid so much as a penny for my work.)

And then once the cattle were all sold, the big shots figured while they were in the selling mood, why stop there? Hell, why not just up and sell the whole godamned ranch and maybe get half rich in the process? (Of course, I do want you to understand that at the time of the big vote to liquidate, cattle prices were at an all-time low and the market for dryland ranch property was the worst it had been in this century.)

You're right, it doesn't take a whole lot of intelligence to see that *that* was a dumb thing to do. But it was no big deal, we figured. After all, Elaine and I had a nice little herd of our own good young cows and a couple of good using-type cow horses. Besides, anybody with good sense could see the ranch wasn't likely to sell for a long time even at the horribly depressed price it would have to be offered for. I had brought enough furniture from Oklahoma to get by on and we figured we could scrounge ourselves a used pickup. A. T. even offered to loan us a stock trailer. The only real difference was that now we'd just be working for ourselves is all—and not busting our asses for other people. It would be a welcome change, right?

Wrong. Seein' as how these people were on such a roll, they went ahead and elected to give Miss Elaine and her husband

134

George Bibb on Satan (about 1920)

thirty days to get their asses off the ranch. Yep, it was another intelligent move . . . just let the place stand empty and fall apart. Either that or rent it out to somebody who would more than likely overgraze it to the point that it would be worthless as grassland for several years thereafter.

I want you to know that all this nearly killed my wife. She had worked long and hard to realize her dream of keeping up her grandfather's ranch. She had succeeded in building up a fine herd of quality cattle with selective breeding, careful culling, and not a small amount of worry, work, and tears. Too, winter was fast approaching, and to be given thirty days to remove cattle would be bad enough for someone with the means to buy or lease pasture—we didn't have those means. Elaine had unselfishly put everything she had into the ranch and the livestock and just as it was finally beginning to pay off. . . .

As much as anything, I think, Elaine was embarrassed—embarrassed that she wasn't going to be able to keep George Bibb's ranch together. And that was hard for her . . . hard because I think keeping the ranch together was something that she regarded as a commitment—indeed, a *promise* she'd made to her late grandfather. It was as though she felt she was letting him down.

Anyway, I'm glad the old gentleman didn't have to be around to see what happened to his ranch. But then I guess that's not entirely true, either—in some ways I wish he *were* here to see . . . I know he'd be proud of Elaine.

NINETEEN

Get 'em up . . . Move 'em out . . .

I KNOW I TOLD YOU HOW HARD IT WAS for me whenever I took Big Red down to the sale, and how she was just a troublesome old cull, at that. So I guess you can imagine how difficult it was when we ended up having to sell off our best animals—animals that were fat and healthy and young. And it was especially difficult since we were forced to sell them off at the whim of a small group of jerks who collectively didn't have the intelligence of a box of rocks. Anyway, we were looking to sell our good cows and we just couldn't see loading them up and taking them down to the weekly livestock auction. And while it's true we weren't offered much time to get ourselves off the place, and a public auction was clearly one solution to having to disperse a number of beef cattle on short notice, we were determined to go that route only if we couldn't get them placed as a herd at private treaty. I guess you could say we looked at the livestock sale as a kind of a junkyard where you took those culls that most knowledgeable cattlefolks wouldn't consider keeping in their herds—you know, old cows with chronically plugged-up spigots, troublesome fence-walking calves . . . that sort of beast.

I'm sure I don't have to tell you that one should never appear as though he's in a hurry to dispose of anything he's looking to sell, be it a used car or a herd of cattle. Which is why I made every effort to sound casual when I mentioned to the guy who ran the feedstore and to the county agent at the courthouse that Elaine and I were kind of thinking of selling our good stock if we could find them a suitable home with somebody who would take them all *as a herd*. And I told our neighbor, Filo Grossman, Jr. Our neighbor promptly showed some interest.

Filo was a pleasant young man who was trying hard to get into the cattle business. He had managed to lease some pasture that bordered Lake Ranch and, in partnership with his father, was picking up other folks' rejects whenever they went through the sale cheap. Naturally he saw our bunch of cows across the fence every time he worked or checked on his own animals, and to be perfectly frank, I suspect that the obvious difference in quality between our fat mamas with their big chunky babies and his sale-yard bargains was apparent even to him. He called me up the same evening I told him we were looking to sell and asked if he might bring Filo, Sr. over the next afternoon to look at our cattle and maybe discuss some terms.

Now, in case you didn't already know it, trading livestock involves a whole different kind of tradition than is involved in buying, say, a new washing machine or a bass boat. I first learned about the tradition back when I was strictly a horse-person. You can say what you will about the used car salesman, but believe me, the horror stories you've heard about horse traders have mostly been true. And the same things go for cow traders—only double. (Remember how Jack traded the family cow for a handful of "magic" beans and, in so doing, nearly caused his poor old silver-haired mother to faint dead away? Well, the feller who made up that story sure enough knew something about cattle traders, even if he did have an over-worked imagination when it came to beanstalks and giants.)

So anyway, when the Filos came over that next day, we went through the whole rural ritual: We drank coffee. We talked about moisture. We talked about the *lack* of moisture. We talked about the price of hay. We mumbled half-heartedly about how badly our common fence needed repair (we were neither of us quite ready to volunteer to get started working on it, however).

We shook our heads and emitted mournful sighs over the sorry state of affairs of the economy in general and the cattle business in particular. We drank some more coffee. We cussed the county for its reluctance to properly grade our roads. And finally we walked out to the branding pens where Elaine and I had early that morning penned up the cattle who were the real object of the Filos' visit.

Filo, Sr. chewed on a match stick as he strolled among our gentle animals and looked them over carefully. After awhile he allowed as how we had us a pretty nice little bunch of cows. (I should add that he allowed this in such a manner that anyone not fluent in livestock traderese would very likely have interpreted his comments to indicate that our cows were actually as sorry a bunch of no-account critters as he'd ever had the misfortune to walk among.) He asked what were we "hoping" to get for them. I named our price and added that there wasn't a whole lot of "hope" to it—that the price we were asking was fair and firm.

Filo, Sr. smiled and shook his head sadly.

"Yeah . . . I can remember back when top pure-bred cattle were worth almost that much money," he said.

After the Filos were gone, I told Elaine that I'd bet her a hundred dollar bill we'd hear from them by noon the next day.

"Why, the old fart's never stood that close to good cows," I laughed. "He'll be pacing around out in front of the bank in the morning hat in hand waiting for them to open the doors."

Filo, Jr. called the next evening. Again, we spent a quarter of an hour talking about rain and the unseemly price of hay.

"By the way," he finally got around to saying. "Me and my dad figure that if you'll throw in your blue heeler cow dog— even though he don't appear to be particularly well trained— that we guess we'll help you and Miss Elaine out and give you-all the goin' market price for your whole herd."

I can accurately report that I did *not* hang up on the sonofabitch. Neither did I resort to unneighborly name-calling. Our telephone conversation, however, was at an end.

In the first place, the cow dog the bastard was referring to was *Lefty,* for Chrissakes! And I doubt seriously that I have to tell you my feelings concerning the prospect of turning my little sidekick over to some dumb redneck in order to get rid of some cows that I wasn't all that anxious to be rid of in the first place. And as for the remark about "market price," I can only say that what this idiot was suggesting was that we weigh the godamn cattle and then he'd offer what the sorryest old cancer-eye killers were bringing at the sale yard down in Clovis.

Early the next morning—and I'm not making this up, either—a young fellow we'd never met called up and said that he and his wife had just acquired a ranch not far from ours and that they were looking to stock it with some good mother cows. He said the county agent in town had given him our name as having some prime native cattle that we wanted to see kept together in a bunch. He came out a couple of days later and spent about ten minutes looking at our herd before he bought every last one of them, where they stood, for the price we were asking.

Okay . . . maybe you're right and the fact this fellow so quickly agreed to our asking price without batting an eye means that we were asking way too little. But I can tell you this: Our cattle were quietly moved less than ten miles to pasture that was a carbon copy of what they'd always known. They weren't hauled a hundred miles in a semi-truck to be jammed into some crowded holding pen and then run through a sale ring while being yelled at and poked and jabbed with electrical cattle prods and hot-shots. No indeed. They stayed together as a herd. Of course when the fellow invited Elaine to come by and visit with Startled and Val and Retardo and the others any time she was in the neighborhood, the tears began to flow and both he and I looked away and cleared our throats and shuffled our boots in the dust uncomfortably.

One other thing while I'm thinking about it. About a week later Filo, Jr. called up. He said he wanted to come over and look at those cows of ours again. I guess maybe he figured he'd

Querry and company

made us sweat long enough and that we'd probably be ready to take his offer.

Now, I liked Filo, Jr. But I'll admit that it was with no small amount of righteous satisfaction that I somewhat condescendingly (I see now) explained to him that the really *good* cattle don't last long on the market and that ours were a lot better than what he was used to and that they had sold within twelve hours of him turning them down. He'd missed his chance is what it was, and he wasn't likely to get another opportunity that good for a long time. I'll admit, too, that I lied and told him that the price we'd quoted him was special because he was our favorite neighbor and that selling them to a stranger had brought us more than five hundred dollars extra, thank you very much. Then I inquired if he'd found himself a good cow dog yet and asked if there'd been any cheap killers go through down at Clovis last week.

TWENTY

Take Me to the Green Valley

IMAGINE IF YOU CAN A WORKING CATTLE ranch with all the livestock removed. Such a place becomes at once a strange and empty place—eerie and ghostlike in many ways.

As you might imagine then, there just wasn't a whole lot to keep us on the ranch once our cattle were all gone. Except as a touchstone for a crazy-quilt mixture of memories good and bad, George Bibb's Lake Ranch had always existed for but one reason . . . as an adequate place to raise and run cows. Now, however, there wasn't anything left for Elaine and me on that place. Not without the livestock, anyway.

I should tell you that my wife and I spent many a sleepless night there toward the end . . . sitting up and drinking coffee at the kitchen table, talking about where we might go . . . what we might do. I know I told you how from the very start Elaine had her mind set on living out her days on that ranch. It was clear to me that all this was breaking her heart and that no matter what we did or where we went it was likely going to be a difficult time for her.

I was educated as a college English teacher. Just like about half a million younger and better connected—in university circles, at least—other job-seekers. Besides, it was late fall and the school year was already under way . . . teaching slots were

filled and faculties had long since been decided upon for that
year. And while it's true I was selling articles to newspapers and
magazines fairly regularly, income from that source was spotty,
at best. And the money I did receive from time to time was far
from adequate for us to live on.

If you've paid close attention to the photographs that illus-
trate this book, you know already that Elaine is a fine photographer. And I recall I told you early on how she had worked
as a newspaper photographer back before taking over the running of her grandfather's ranch. And I'd come to count on her
skills from time to time when some uppity editor demanded
good quality photographs to accompany some article I'd been
assigned. So while Elaine worried that she was perhaps a little
rusty, we were hoping that maybe she could get a job with a
newspaper. Income from that, then—combined with a concen-
trated effort on my part to settle down and work on and sell
my writing—just might tide us over until I could find honest
work, or at least a teaching position at a college somewhere.

The trouble with that reasoning, of course, was that any
place I might conceivably find a teaching position and where
Elaine might also locate a daily newspaper large enough that it
could use one more photographer was almost certain to be in
some noisy, polluted, overpopulated, mugger-infested metro-
politan area. Clearly, any reasonable individual would face up to
the fact that he was just going to have to pack up and head out
for L.A., or New York, or Dallas, or Albuquerque at the very
least. Certainly I've been accused of a lot of things, but I confess that being reasonable is not one of them. I figured that
Elaine had taken a big chance taking me on as a ranch hand
with so little to recommend me, and now, with the tables
turned, she needed as much as anything for me to be strong and
purposeful as we settled on our new direction.

So in the middle of one of those sleepless nights in Novem-
ber, I poured Miss Elaine another cup of coffee and announced
that if a band of mean and spiteful no-accounts could unjustly
force a wife of mine from her rightful home, and if as a result
the two of us were, with very little warning, now going to

have to try to figure out a way to make our living doing something altogether different from what we were very happily and ably doing before, we could at least by-god look at it as an opportunity for high adventure and do it in some place that we figured we'd really like to be.

That night we determined that we'd move to Taos.

Taos—it rhymes with *house*—is a small and pleasant town in Northern New Mexico that relies pretty much on winter skiers and sunburned summer tourists as its primary industry. With that in mind, you probably won't be surprised to learn that Taos has no major university campus. Therefore the likelihood of my resuming a teaching career there was slim. Taos does, however, have a newspaper . . . an award-winning once-a-week publication that boasts an editorial staff of something like four poorly paid but top-notch full-time journalists. So you see the chance of Elaine just showing up and hiring on as their star reporter and chief photographer right off the bat seemed highly unlikely, as well. And on top of all that, the most recent figures I'd seen published in that newspaper showed Taos County suffering from a whopping 33 percent unemployment rate!

Unlike Santa Rosa, Taos is set in one of the most beautiful places on earth. At an altitude of 7,000 feet, it lies in a green valley of the Sangre de Cristo Mountain range. The town is nestled at the base of the magnificently forested Taos Mountain to the north and is bordered to the west by a high desert mesa cracked down its middle by the awesomely jagged and spectacular Rio Grande gorge.

You might like to know that Taos does not have a Stuckey's or a Truckstops of America. (Come to think of it, as far as I know none of the restaurants in Taos sell diesel fuel.) On the other hand, Taos does have a half-dozen bookstores and three (count 'em, THREE) honest-to-god supermarkets, one of which sells live lobsters! Oh sure, you're probably saying to yourself that you've heard there's a store on the town plaza that advertises rubber tomahawks imported from Taiwan, and it's true a call to the Taos County Chamber of Commerce will reveal that there's not a fancy country club like they have over in Santa Rosa. And even though a lot of folks would consider it almost un-American considering it's a town that attracts tourists, Taos is not even close to an Interstate highway.

But Taos is still considered an important cultural, art, and literary center. In fact, as I understand it, Taos is something like the third leading art center in the entire free world . . . outdone only by Paris and New York and sort of tied neck and neck with San Francisco. (Art-lovers from Santa Fe claim *that* town is number three, but I say that's just a case of over-zealous boosterism, and dismiss it out of hand.)

Mind you, Elaine and I didn't exactly discover Taos all on our own, and I don't want to give you that impression. Lots of important people knew about the place before we did. For example, most literate teen-age boys of my generation secretly read portions of *Lady Chatterley's Lover,* and those of us who didn't go blind or crazy on account of having done so grew up to discover that the author of that learned book, D. H. Lawrence, lived in Taos for a while—indeed, his ashes are enshrined on the Lawrence Ranch north of town. I probably don't have to tell you who's buried in the Taos cemetery named in honor of famous frontiersman and Indian scout Kit Carson any more than I have to tell you who's buried in Grant's Tomb. And of course, as any flower child turned stockbroker can tell you, Easy Rider Dennis Hopper used to live in a big house in Taos. Every art lover knows that flamboyant Navajo artist R. C. Gorman lives just up the road in a house with a giant indoor swimming pool. And two-steppin' honkey-tonk frequenters probably know that heart-throb C & W singer-songwriter Michael Martin Murphey makes his home in Taos and even has a fancy cowboy and Indian shop on the plaza. Book author and Academy Award–winning screenwriter John Nichols lives nearby in a wonderfully cluttered adobe house *without* a swimming pool (or an indoor toilet, for that matter). And of course the Taos Pueblo was ancient long before the first adobe brick was laid in the town of Taos. Standing essentially outside of time, the

Pueblo has been continuously occupied for something approaching seven hundred years.

Elaine and I found a seventy-five-year-old adobe house on three-quarters of an acre at the foot of Taos Mountain. The house has two fireplaces—one each in the living room and in what's become the study—and there's a really great pot-bellied stove in the bedroom. We don't have a swimming pool (we do have indoor plumbing). Our front porch—the *portal*, it's called—looks out across the valley and the lights of the town. The living room window frames the burning sunsets over the gorge. And from our bedroom window we can see across Indian pastureland—dotted with horses and cows and, yes, buffalo—to the Mountain. We consider it a rare privilege to live in the midst of such incredible beauty.

Moving is never very much fun, I think. The actual packing up and loading and unloading and cleaning out closets and trying to decide what to take and what to get rid of . . . that part of moving is not one of my favorite things to do. But I was excited at the prospect of a new place and life, and I was anxious to get on with it. Elaine was nervous and understandably unsure of what lay ahead. She tried to put up a brave front, but this was all a little scary for her, I knew.

There were still some loose ends to tie up, of course. The two borrowed geldings Rumshop and Moonshine had to be sent back to their owners—Rumshop to a ranch near Fort Sumner and old Moonshine retired to pasture with a band of mares in the South Valley of Albuquerque. We worked out a deal with Filo, Jr. to board Elaine's mare Josie and her two colts until we could find pasture somewhere around Taos. And I already told you about the old mare Comet.

We made the move in four trips with a cattle trailer. The dogs thought the whole thing was a great and happy adventure, especially when they discovered that until I could get around to fencing a run for them they got to stay in the house.

The cats were not so pleased. Living out on the ranch, a great distance from any neighbors who might have pets, we never had to be particularly concerned with having our cats neutered—as long as all our cats were of the same sex, of course. However, the town dwellers among you will not be surprised to learn that such was not the case for us now that we had to contend with roaming bands of ill-mannered tomcats who apparently had no trouble whatsoever in determining right away that Fearless and Kiki were attractive young females even though I did still refer to Fearless as "he."

Naturally we had to keep the cats indoors when we first moved so that they might get used to where home was before being turned out to hunt birds and whatever else it is that cats do. Elaine and I were distressed when both of them took the opportunity of being the new girls in town to come into heat together and begin immediately the most blatant and disgusting displays of sexual receptiveness imaginable. (I guess that's one of those other things cats do.) Not only would they lurk around the doors awaiting an opportunity to dart outside to welcome their squalling nocturnal gentlemen callers, but they engaged in the sleaziest of displays toward Lefty. (I account for this by the fact that the feelings the cats were experiencing were, I suppose, as new and baffling to them as they were to me.) To his credit, I should add, Lefty always looked shocked and humiliated when Fearless began to purr seductively and wave his rear end in Lefty's face.

The local veterinarian announced that he couldn't spay the girls while they were in heat so we had to wait out their entire cycle. Then when we took them in for their surgery, the guy allowed as how it would cost us $110 to have the two cats fixed! I coughed and sputtered and told him did I look like I'd just rode into town on a green chile truck and that I thought that was a bit steep for a couple of found alley cats and that I by-god knew how to castrate bull calves and I believed I'd just sharpen up my good pocket knife and do the job myself. Elaine reminded me what had happened last time I'd tried to operate on one of her cats and I forked over the ransom money.

One morning about a week after we'd arrived in Taos—as soon as we'd gotten halfway settled into the house—Elaine got together a portfolio of her best photographs and went into town to visit with the editor of the *Taos News*. Dressed in her best new skirt and blouse, her dark hair shining and perfectly arranged, Elaine was prettier than any picture she carried that morning. There was a terrible lump in my throat and everything got blurry as I stood in the drive and waved as she drove off toward the plaza. We'd been married just two years—and all the things that had been so important to Elaine when I first came into her life were gone, it seemed.

A hundred and twenty miles to the south, Lake Ranch stood empty and abandoned; it stands empty today. Since the day we pulled away from the front gate with the last trailer load, Elaine's never once been back to the place—I doubt seriously that she ever will return. The cattle are all gone. So are the horses. . . .

Watching Elaine go off looking for a job that morning I felt guilty . . . as though I were somehow responsible for a great loss in her life. More than anything else in the world right then, I wanted Elaine to feel good about what we were setting out to do . . . I wanted my wife to be happy in this new place.

It's almost a commonplace among locals that Taos Mountain is the central symbol in the lives of all those of us who live in its shadow. It's as simple as that. The Taos Indians believe their Mountain to be sacred—their creation myth places the Mountain's Blue Lake as the very spot from which their ancestors emerged into this world. And so it is for them the holiest of places.

And there's a saying in Taos, that the Mountain either accepts or rejects people who try to live at its base. There are no two ways about it . . . if the Mountain doesn't want you here, it won't allow you to remain. I believe that to be true.

I'm happy to tell you that Elaine began to work part-time for the *Taos News* as a reporter/photographer the week after that

The Mountain from our back yard

first morning she met with the editor. A couple of months later she was working full-time as the paper's chief photographer.

Friends often ask me privately if she's gotten over leaving her beloved ranch. I tell them about how when we're driving through town Elaine will tell me—just out of the blue—how much she loves living in Taos . . . she calls it *her town*. And I tell them how some of my favorite moments are those times when she'll come up behind me when I'm at my desk or reading in front of the fire—how the Beautiful Young Rancher Lady hugs my neck and tells me how much she loves our house. I want you to know that I honestly don't believe Elaine has ever been happier than she is today.

Yeah, things have worked out very nicely for us here, thank you very much. A couple of weeks after Elaine got on at the *Taos News,* I signed on with the University of New Mexico

Press to publish this book. And right now, as soon as I finish a couple more sentences here, I'm going to get up and go into town to the post office and mail this last chapter off to Albuquerque. Then I believe I'll take Lefty and Domino for a walk, and begin outlining a new book I've been thinking about lately.

I do believe the Mountain likes us.

Afterword

MY FRIEND LEFTY WAS A COW DOG—
he simply loved to work cattle. But when we left the range and
moved to town, he adapted quickly and easily and was happy.
And later when we began a period of much travel, Lefty took a
great and immediate liking to life on the road.

Our travels took us throughout the southwestern United
States and farther still into Mexico. Along the way, Lefty ex-
plored cliff dwellings and Anasazi ruins and watched dances and
rodeos on the Navajo and Jicarilla Apache Reservations. In
Texas, he peed in the Pedernales River just upstream from the
Lyndon B. Johnson Ranch, and in California, at my urging I'll
confess, pooped in the sand near Richard Nixon's home in San
Clemente. In Utah he was unjustly harassed by a chickenshit
park ranger at Arches National Monument, and he was sprayed
by skunks and visited by coyotes in Oklahoma. And I want you
to know that Lefty loved every moment of it all.

Mexico was especially exciting to Lefty. He found the sights
and smells there exotic and wonderful. It was in Mexico—in
Matehuala in the state of San Luis Potosí—that Lefty encoun-
tered the dog with bright purple splotches painted on its body
and a large yellow plastic bucket over its head. (The purple
splotches were the result of someone's having painted the animal
with gentian violet wound dressing; the yellow bucket, its bot-

tom cut out and slipped over the dog's head like a megaphone, was a makeshift device meant to prevent the animal from licking some part of itself so that the bright purple medicine might work its cure on the rash or wound or whatever it was that afflicted it.) All his life Lefty was interested in other dogs, and the first dog he saw in this land of exotic and exciting smells was walking around with a bucket on its head. What's more, this particular dog was walking around real proud-like, as though that was just the way dogs naturally went around south of the border. Lefty was literally struck dumb by this spectacle. It took him days to recover his composure. And for weeks afterward we'd see him sitting alone—glassy-eyed and staring into space. I like to imagine that he was remembering the bucket-headed dog back in Matehuala.

After Mexico we spent a few months in western Oklahoma in a small farming town where Elaine had inherited some land from her grandfather. It was not a particularly good time in our lives—it was an unusually cold winter and, with the exception of a couple of good folks there, we were viewed with suspicion as outsiders in the community.

For one thing, we used to take walks. And in case you don't know it, I will tell you that Oklahoma farmers—those around Butler, Oklahoma, at least—are not inclined to walk more than a dozen steps if their pickups will start. So the four of us—Elaine and me and Lefty and Domino—were somewhat conspicuous in our habit of walking three or four miles a day. Sometimes we'd take our walks around a lake that was several miles distant and so would ride over in the truck. The boys—Lefty and Domino—especially liked those times. Then they got to ride and walk.

I remember one cold afternoon when I let down the tailgate for the dogs; instead of jumping easily in as was his habit, Lefty jumped three times into the *side* of the truck, falling each time into a heap and looking baffled. I remember I called him something other than his name—"stupid" probably—and picked him up and tossed him roughly into the bed of the truck.

Later, walking along the trail by the lake, Lefty kept running into my legs, nearly tripping me. And when the boys were running loose in a pasture and I whistled them in, Lefty uncharacteristically ignored me. I'm sorry to tell you that I scolded him again.

Within three days my little friend was completely blind. He would walk into walls, and he couldn't find his food dish. When I took him outside and would speak to him, he clearly was unable to determine the direction from which my voice was coming. But he'd decide that I was "over there" somewhere—more often than not he was wrong—and take off running like the healthy dog he'd so recently been, running into a fence or tree or some other obstacle unless I could get him to me first.

The veterinarians in the nearest town were, I believe, well equipped and good at their work. I know that they were genuinely caring and gentle with my dog. One of the vets met a near-frantic Elaine and me at three o'clock one morning after Domino had awakened us to discover Lefty in violent convulsions. The vets X-rayed and blood-tested and did, I have to think, all that they knew how to do. They concluded that it was a brain tumor of some kind, that nothing could be done, and that it would not get better, only worse.

Had Lefty been merely blind, I know we could have managed, him and me. But he couldn't hear, and he couldn't eat. I don't know if my dog was hurting—I do know I was—but I know that he was frightened. One evening, realizing when I was petting him that I was sitting in a chair, Lefty crawled up into my lap and lay quietly for several minutes. Lefty would never get on furniture—much less my lap.

Elsewhere in this book I've said that Lefty devoted his days to making my life fuller and less lonely. I have to feel that he knew I loved him, but I'll always regret that I didn't work nearly as hard as he did at showing it.

We said our good-byes early one morning in a vet clinic at Arapaho, Oklahoma. Certainly no place would have been good for those good-byes, but so many places would have been better.

Lefty was six years old.

Ron Querry

Tucson, Arizona
September 21, 1993